"Rich Stevenson has given us a gift i
from it. It is fresh in expression ar
riences Rich shares are down-to-ear
day walk as Christians. If you dor
page, you will certainly find yours_____apter. The
fact that Rich shares his own walk—his struggles and failures
as well as his confidence and victories—gives authenticity
and power to his message. It is obvious that he has been
gripped by grace and the message he seeks to share. His passion comes through in his writing and personal witness. He
wills one thing: to make the secrets of the spiritual life so clear
and inviting that we will own them for ourselves."

—Maxie D. Dunnam, president, Asbury Theological Seminary

"An exuberant joy and playful excitement permeates this book.
It is filled with insights that will enrich your spiritual life.
Above all, as Rich Stevenson unpacks the 'one thing' passages,
get ready for a fresh encounter with Jesus, the risen Lord!"

—Stephen Seamands, professor of Christian doctrine,
Asbury Theological Seminary

"I loved it! Rich's uncomplicated fresh bread style keeps pulling
you into the flow to discover '. . . the simplicity and purity of
devotion to Christ' (2 Cor. 11:3). What delights me most is the
lack of effort to naturalize God so the reader can better understand God from the human perspective. Rich simply allows
for the mystery of the majesty of God to prevail. His style pro-
vides abundant opportunity to revel in our Father."

—Paul Bersche, senior pastor,
Restoration Christian Fellowship

"The problem of double-mindedness—of trying to serve two
masters, as Jesus put it—is one of the greatest challenges facing followers of Christ today. So much calls for our attention
and demands constant consideration. In simple and compelling
terms, Rich Stevenson explores the biblical fundamentals for
developing a singular focus and an all-consuming purpose.

Born out of his own search for 'this one thing,' Rich draws on the resources of his Christian heritage and the lessons learned as a husband and father while pioneering a Great Commission, world mission church movement. With refreshing and intimate transparency, he opens the doors to the secrets of the Spirit-enabled life of a twenty-first-century pilgrim."

—David Gyertson, Ph.D., president, Taylor University

"In a world of overload and cultural clutter, the Scriptures point to basic kingdom essentials. With wit and clarity Rich Stevenson explores the few things that really matter. This is a helpful read about core truth."

—Mark Nysewander, pastor, Bethany Missionary Church

"We are all being called back—back from the hype and noise of a media-saturated world, back from the haste and confusion of the babbling and bumbling of a truth compromising culture, back to the worthy, the durable and the wise—to the eternal. To God. Here's a resource to help us find the way to the genuine and lasting."

—Jack W. Hayford, pastor, The Church On the Way;
Chancellor, The King's Seminary

"I love Rich Stevenson's ability to make the Gospel stories come alive! His insights are both humorous and thought provoking. When he talks about the woman taken in adultery or the man born blind, you feel as though you were there. I especially like the way he approaches our need to emphasize the Holy Spirit. He takes a topic that for many is difficult and, through his own transparency and sincerity, presents it in a very clear and effective way."

—Tom Tanner

Secrets
of the
Spiritual Life

10 LESSONS FROM THE
"ONE THING" PASSAGES

Rich Stevenson

Baker Books
A Division of Baker Book House Co
Grand Rapids, Michigan 49516

Published by Baker Books
a division of Baker Book House Company
P.O. Box 6287, Grand Rapids, MI 49516-6287
www.bakerbooks.com

Printed in the United States of America

Library of Congress Cataloging-in-Publication Data

Stevenson, Rich, 1963–
    Secrets of the spiritual life : 10 lessons from the "one thing" passages / Richard Stevenson.
        p.   cm.
    Includes bibliographical references.
    ISBN 0-8010-6448-1 (pbk.)
    1. Spiritual life—Biblical teaching. I. Title.
BS680.S7 .S84 2003
248.4—dc21   2002152040

Not a single person who knows my family would deny that I am blessed beyond measure! I would like this book to open with a few words dedicated to the ones that represent God's most wonderful gift:

Tania—I love you because of your deep and growing pursuit of Jesus. I love that you have been patient with me. I love your commitment to our home and our children. I love your willingness to risk with me, and your support and encouragement of the vision. I love that your smile, your eyes, and your walk still make my heart pound after twenty years.

Zachary, Jacob, Jessie, and Corrie—You can't possibly know how proud I am of each of you! I love that you love Jesus; there is nothing more important. I love how each of you contribute to our ministry and have sacrificed for the cause. I love what I see each of you becoming. Thank you for continuing to fill our lives with joy and laughter.

Contents

Acknowledgments

I am so grateful for such loving and Christlike parents, Harry and Ann Stevenson, who model faithfulness not only in marriage but in ministry as well. Thank you for leading the way. Your children do rise up to call you "blessed."

I am privileged to pastor the most exciting church I've ever attended. Most Sundays I am overwhelmed at the thought that "I get to preach here!" Thank you, Great Commission Fellowship, for giving me time to write. Thank you Ron and Phil for standing with me from the very beginning. I can't imagine doing this without you. And thank you, GCF staff and leadership, for your tireless commitment and joyful pursuit of Jesus. Two words: Hold on . . . the ride has just begun!

What a joy it is to have such a large and extended family! Our life is sweeter because of the Hunters, the Bules, the Moores, the Newtons, the Vogels and Furdas, the Houps, the Jacksons, and FFH.

Steve and Pam English, thanks for providing the place and time for me to outline this book. It was surely the presence of Jesus in your home for at-risk kids in

Guatemala that brought focus to my heart. The ambiance in that hotel in the center of Antigua didn't hurt either. I felt like Hemingway!

Our family is eternally grateful for Trinity Church International in Omaha, Nebraska. Thank you for giving a great gift of hospitality during our sabbatical. Your generosity provided the setting not only to write this book but to reconnect with my family. It was fruit that will last.

I am very grateful for the wonderful help I received from Melissa Ingram in preparing this manuscript for publication. I am sure it would not have had a second look without your effort. It has also been pure joy to work with Baker Books and especially Vicki Crumpton, Kelley Sytsma, and Karen Steele. Your insight and wisdom, as well as your delightful interaction, make me wonder if the stories I've heard about editors are true!

I am a better pastor and leader because of some guys I watch who lead the way I want to lead. Thanks Cecil, Rodney, Mark, Les, Tom, and Anthony.

Last word . . . Jake, you better start reading!

Foreword

"Martha," said Jesus, according to the Gospel story, "you are distracted with many things." This good woman, intent on serving Jesus and her guests well, was anxious, literally "pulled apart" (for that is the root meaning of *distracted*). So Jesus gently chided her, "One thing is needful."

And that word is for us, for we too are often distracted people, pulled apart by the multiplying choices of our world, tensed by the pace of change.

In *The Lexus and the Olive Tree*, writer Thomas Friedman says that technological change and instant communication are creating two worlds—the "fast" world and the "slow" world, determined by varied responses to globalization. In a later piece, he reports on an economic conference where corporate life was described as going faster and faster with less and less time for family, friendship, and play. "This sounds like a description of hell," burst out the chairman of SONY America!

Perhaps in a faster world, we need a slower church!

But distraction is not only the occupational hazard of secular life. Some time ago, pastor/writer Eugene

11

Peterson wrote that he never read letters addressed to a "busy pastor," because the terms were contradictory! Yet we too, clergy or laity, get chewed up and distracted. We are, most of us if we are honest, latter-day Marthas.

Rich Stevenson has sensed this. And out of his own full life, he has discovered (or rediscovered) that the secret is not in the circumference (merely reducing activities) but at the center (refocusing our hearts).

I first came to know Rich when he was part of our Arrow Leadership Program. I sensed his passion, admired his vision. The score of his life has already had many notes: evangelist, pastor, church planter, mission activist. But increasingly he has sought to find the theme of his life in the "one thing"—to have an undivided heart toward God.

His reflections from Scripture and life on the pregnant phrase "one thing" are helpful and practical. They point us to the way of power and fruitfulness. And they challenge us not to settle for being busy people but to seek to be deep people.

One thing I would suggest. Do not rush through this book. Read it slowly. Linger on the special words that speak to your own life and lifestyle. Let it lead you to heed the quiet voice that says to you as it did to Martha: One thing is necessary. And, like Mary, choose what is best.

Dr. Leighton Ford
Charlotte, North Carolina

The Essentials

Maybe you have seen the movie *City Slickers* starring Billy Crystal and Jack Palance. Billy Crystal plays a white-collar guy named Mitch. He is married with children and is questioning whether or not there's anything really important about his life. He and two other friends decide to "vacation" out West and take part in a cattle drive. Jack Palance plays a mysterious and intimidating cowboy named Curly, who wears a black hat and a red bandana. He leads this bunch of city slickers with gruff reluctance.

In one scene, Curly and Mitch are riding together. Because Mitch has suppressed his fear and made a stand against him, Curly has warmed up to him. With a cigarette hanging out of the corner of his mouth, Curly says, "A cowboy leads a different kind of life . . . when there were cowboys. We're a dying breed. A couple of days, we'll move this herd across the river, drive on through the valley. . . . There's nothing like bringin' in the herd!"

Mitch responds, "That's great! Your life makes sense to you!"

Curly laughs.

Mitch says, "What's so funny?"

Curly looks right into Mitch's eyes. "You city folks, you worry about a lot of *stuff!*" (*Stuff* is not the actual word in the movie. He's an intimidating cowboy, after all.) "How old are you, thirty-eight?"

Mitch replies, "Thirty-nine."

"Yeah, you all come up here around the same age, same problems. You spend about fifty weeks a year getting knots in your rope, and then, and then you think two weeks up here will untie 'em for you. None of you get it! Do you know what the secret of life is?"

"No, what?" Mitch asks.

"This . . ." Curly then lifts his index finger up.

Mitch says, "Your finger?"

Curly responds, "One thing . . . just one thing. You stick to that and everything else don't mean *squat!*" (Again, not really the word, I apologize. Curly's really gruff!)

Mitch then asks the essential question: "That's great, but what's the one thing?"

Curly smiles, shifts his cigarette, and says, "That's what you've got to figure out!"

I've got good news for you. You don't have to go out West to figure out what the "one thing" is! All through Scripture, God has inspired passages that give us the real essence of spiritual life. This book will draw your attention to eight of these passages. All of them, taken from the NIV, have "one thing" in common: They all con-

14

tain the words "one thing." Remember some of these passages? David sings, "One thing I ask of the Lord." Paul declares, "One thing I do." Peter charges, "Don't forget this one thing!" And Jesus tenderly instructs, "One thing is needed."

I believe that you will find the secrets of the spiritual life in these eight "one thing" passages. Let me make *several* promises: (1) there will be no more references where I will have to clean up the language, (2) this book is a lot easier on your hindquarters than a cattle drive, and (3) if you will let him, the Holy Spirit will speak through God's Word. Oh, one more thing, I'd like to think that this book might help "get the knots out of your rope"!

Eternity

One thing I ask of the LORD,
    this is what I seek:
that I may dwell in the house of the LORD
    all the days of my life.

Psalm 27:4

I want to know one thing, the way to heaven.

John Wesley

In mansions of glory and endless delight,
I'll ever adore Thee in heaven so bright;
I'll sing with the glittering crown on my brow;
If ever I loved Thee, my Jesus, 'tis now.

William R. Featherston

It was a dinner I will never forget. Well, it wasn't actually the meal. It was what took place after the meal. What we did after the meal wasn't really unusual, but what happened that night changed my life! After dinner my father led our family in devotions, which he did every night. Typically it was something I would persevere through. Here's the routine: My father would read the devotional; we would then go around the table as my mother, my two older sisters, my father, and I would all say something we were thankful for; and then my dad would close in prayer. It all sounds wonderful, but I was six years old, and every weekday, right after dinner, I had an appointment with destiny. I would get my mother to safety pin a towel around my neck, and then it would come on TV . . . "Nanna, nanna, nanna, nanna . . . BATMAN!" Every night, I was there with them . . . "smack!" . . . "pow!" . . . "bang!" . . . the caped crusaders. That's why it was so difficult to get through family devotions.

But this night was different. My father read the devotional for that day. It was about heaven. After he finished reading it, he began talking from his own understanding of Scripture about the wonders of heaven. He talked about the streets of gold. Can you imagine a place where they pave the streets with gold? He described gates of pearl and a sea that sparkled. He said heaven would have Bible heroes whom we could talk to and loved ones to be reunited with. He spoke of a place where people wouldn't be sick anymore and where no one would even think to cry. "The best thing of all," he said, "is that Jesus will be there!" As he shared, his eyes filled up with tears. He ended with this statement: "Won't it be great to be a family together in heaven!"

Something ignited in me, feelings I had never had before. At first it was excitement about the wonders of heaven; then a different feeling caused my stomach to go into knots. I was aware of my sin. For the first time, a realization hit me: Something needs to happen to me if I am going to go to heaven. I also felt a deep longing. I wanted more than anything else to be in heaven with my family. My father was upstairs preparing for a church meeting. I went to him and said, "Daddy, I don't think I am going to go to heaven!" He didn't seem surprised. He explained some more about Jesus, how he died on a cross for my sins. Then he knelt with me at my bed and helped me to invite Jesus into my heart.

That night was real! Something changed in me. Jesus came into my heart and I felt it. Looking back I know that this is what I was created for, a relationship with the Father. That night I did have an appointment with destiny! Each one of us has been created for this experience. A longing for eternity is built into us. Augustine referred to this as "a God-shaped vacuum." The closer we get to God, the more intense this longing to be with him becomes.

David expresses this longing in Psalm 27:4: "One thing I ask of the LORD, this is what I seek: that I may dwell in the house of the LORD all the days of my life." David understood his destiny. He knew what he had been created for. In Psalm 23 he wrote, "Surely goodness and love will follow me all the days of my life, and I will dwell in the house of the LORD forever" (v. 6). He was created for eternity, and the deep longing of his soul was to be with his God—forever. For David, eternity was his Father's house. Moses understood this; he prayed in Psalm 90:1, "Lord, you have been our home since the beginning" (NCV). Jesus promised this when he said, "If my people love me, they will obey my teaching. My Father will love them, and we will come to them and make our home with them" (John 14:23 NCV). Max Lucado emphasizes God's desire for our fellowship:

God *wants* to be your dwelling place. He has no interest in being a weekend getaway or a Sunday bungalow or a summer cottage. Don't consider using God as a vacation cabin or an eventual retirement home. He wants you under his roof now and always. He wants to be your mailing address, your point of reference; he wants to be your home.[1]

Why would we want to live anywhere else than with "our Father in heaven"? Why would we choose any other dwelling place than his? Why do so many of us live our lives consumed by such lesser and lower passions? Those who are like David long for *one thing* above all else—to dwell in the house of the Lord. And they aren't passionate about God's home because the streets are fourteen-karat and the sea sparkles with rainbow colors. They aren't filled with deep yearnings for heaven because David will be the ultimate worship leader and will probably have backup musicians like Bach and singers like DC Talk. They're not focused on "mansions just over the hilltop." Those who are like David have one consuming passion: to be with the Father, to never leave him. They have already begun their eternity. They have entered into the real essence of heaven's best—being in the presence of our Father. And they have found the pursuit of him to be inexhaustible. The closer you get to the Father, the more intense your longing to be with him becomes!

Listen to the passion in David's voice for the presence of the Lord as he sings:

Better is one day in your courts
than a thousand elsewhere;
I would rather be a doorkeeper in the house of my God
than dwell in the tents of the wicked.

Psalm 84:10

You've got an appointment with destiny. It's what you have been created for. You are built for eternity with God the Father, and it's not only the glitter of heaven, it's living in him right now. "And this is eternal life, that they may know You, the only true God, and Jesus Christ whom You have sent" (John 17:3 NKJV). David wrote in Psalm 16:11, "You have made known to me the path of life; you will fill me with joy in your presence, with eternal pleasures at your right hand." The original Hebrew in that passage is more literally translated, "With your face is fullness of joy, in your right hand are eternal pleasures."

That's what we're talking about! The presence and the pleasures of the Lord. If you have been married for any length of time at all, you know that a multitude of words can be communicated in just one look. When I come into our home, I can tell whether I belong in the high and lofty places or whether I need to dwell with the contrite, just by the look on my wife, Tania's, face! After twenty years of marriage, we know each other. Our Father longs for you to know him intimately. He longs for you to see and know his face and to receive his joy and his eternal pleasure from that intimacy.

For three years prior to planting the church I now pastor, I traveled as an evangelist. I was away from home a lot, separated from my wife and children. I missed so much of their lives. When I was home, I especially loved the evening rituals. One evening when my daughter Jessica was four years old, I got her ready for bed. Unfortunately for her, bedtime was much earlier than she thought it was going to be. She was "ticked" at me. We made it through the teeth cleaning and hair brushing, but she was not happy. I got right into bed with her to pray. Typically we would lay nose to nose with each other and talk about the day. I looked into her big brown eyes and said, "Jessie, I love you." She responded quickly,

"Daddy, I don't love you!" I didn't say anything to her. I just turned my face away from her face. I held my head turned away from her for maybe sixty seconds. It seemed like an eternity. All of a sudden, from deep within her, with tears streaming down her face, she cried out to me, "Daddy, I said I didn't love you, but I do love you! I do love you!"

She couldn't bear that I had turned my face. She had lost my presence and desperately wanted it back.

You've been created for face-to-face intimacy with your Father in heaven. David knew that this was *the* essential thing in life. *One thing,* above all else, I want to dwell in the Father's house. Why? Psalm 27:4 continues, "to gaze upon the beauty of the LORD." David wanted the face of God!

Maybe your sin has caused the Father to turn his face. The Bible says that our holy God still can't look upon our sin. Should you cower in it, hide in shame, or work as hard as you can to clean yourself up? No. You are a breath away from his presence. In repentance breathe the word *mercy* and watch how quickly our Father turns his face.

You've got the chance to begin eternity now. Live in God, know the fullness of joy that is in his face and the eternal pleasures that are in his right hand. This is your appointment with destiny!

Not long ago, I noticed a name written in my Bible . . . Mrs. Markwell . . . in the margin of Psalm 91. What a powerful example of a woman who "dwelled in God" and enjoyed the beauty and joy of his presence. I was a young seminary student doing my supervised ministry at Central Baptist Hospital in Lexington, Kentucky. She was a patient in critical condition for heart trouble; she was elderly and blind. I visited her every day, not because I was providing significant help for her but because she was such a joy to be with. The presence of God was all over her. During that season of ministry, our second son was born in the same hospital. When Mrs. Markwell found out that my son was downstairs, she instructed a family member to bring one of her homemade dolls from home and she gave it to me for Jacob.

Each day I visited her, we would talk and then I would read a passage of Scripture and pray for her. One afternoon all heaven broke loose in that room. I began reading Psalm 91 and before I could finish the first verse, she began reciting it with me from memory. I was caught a little off guard, so I stopped at the second verse. She kept right on going . . . the whole psalm from memory, only stopping once.

> He who dwells in the shelter of the Most High will rest
>   in the shadow of the Almighty.
> I will say of the LORD, "He is my refuge and my
>   fortress,
>   my God, in whom I trust."
> Surely he will save you from the fowler's snare
>   and from the deadly pestilence.
> He will cover you with his feathers,
>   and under his wings you will find refuge;
>   his faithfulness will be your shield and rampart.
> You will not fear the terror of night,
>   nor the arrow that flies by day,
> nor the pestilence that stalks in the darkness,
>   nor the plague that destroys at midday.
> A thousand may fall at your side,
>   ten thousand at your right hand,
>   but it will not come near you.
> You will only observe with your eyes
>   and see the punishment of the wicked.
> If you make the Most High your dwelling—
>   even the LORD, who is my refuge—
> then no harm will befall you,
>   no disaster will come near your tent.

For he will command his angels concerning you
    to guard you in all your ways; . . .

At this verse, she stopped reciting the psalm for just a moment. She smiled big and said, "I like that one!" Then she continued:

. . . they will lift you up in their hands,
    so that you will not strike your foot against a stone.
You will tread upon the lion and the cobra;
    you will trample the great lion and the serpent.
"Because he loves me," says the LORD, "I will rescue
    him;
    I will protect him, for he acknowledges my name.
He will call upon me, and I will answer him;
    I will be with him in trouble,
    I will deliver him and honor him.
With long life will I satisfy him
    and show him my salvation."

I was sitting right by her bed, holding her hand and wiping my tears. I had never heard anything so beautiful and real in all my life. A sister of Mrs. Markwell's was in the far corner of the room. After Mrs. Markwell finished, there was silence. I felt a heaviness, not the heaviness of sorrow but of glory. Within seconds of her last words, Mrs. Markwell took a deep breath and then a long exhale. She was gone.

I froze in place. Her sister rushed over and then she ran to the hallway and pulled a nurse into the room. That nurse immediately took over. She pointed me to a corner of the room, called for more assistance, and then got right on top of Mrs. Markwell—actually straddled her—and began shouting, "Mrs. Markwell, can you hear me, can you hear me?" She breathed into her mouth and then continued shouting. Eventually—it seemed like an hour but was only a moment—Mrs. Markwell opened her eyes and breathed. Do you know what her first words to the nurses were?

"Why didn't you let me go, girls, why didn't you let me go?"

What a woman . . . what a life! She dwelled in the shelter of the Most High and rested in the shadow of the Almighty. By now, I'm sure, she is gazing upon his beauty in glory. That day I saw eternity. It was as real as the hospital bed she lay on. Eternity wasn't far off, some distant land just over the Jordan; it was right there. She lived in it and she pulled me into it. Eternity, the house of God, the beauty of his face, the joy of his eternal pleasure, the glory of his presence. You've been created for this. It is your destiny.

Trust

One thing God has spoken,
   two things have I heard:
that you, O God, are strong,
   and that you, O LORD, are loving.

Psalm 62:11–12

After thousands of hours of prayer and meditation over the intervening years, I can state unequivocally that childlike surrender in trust is the defining spirit of authentic discipleship.

Brennan Manning, *Ruthless Trust*

The brand-new Luce Center had recently been built on the campus of Asbury College in Wilmore, Kentucky. We had heard the murmurings around our little town about this new, state-of-the-art physical education building. In our two stoplight town, the lure of this building captivated us. My boys, Zachary and Jacob, were at that time ages nine and six, and all they could talk about was the new Olympic-size pool with a low dive and a high dive. They knew that the community was invited to use the building for free prior to the official membership plan being established. Their pursuit of that pool was relentless. Finally I gave in and took my sons. I have to admit, the building and the pool were quite impressive!

Zachary took right to the pool and soon was diving off the diving board right into the deep end. Jacob, on the other hand, stayed pretty close to the edge in the shallow end. I could tell by the way he watched his older brother, Jacob was not satisfied with his shallow experience. Several times he got out of the pool and walked toward the board, only to return to the shallow water, afraid to take the plunge. The time for our community swim was limited. Knowing we would have to leave shortly, I said to Jacob, "You don't have to go off that diving board, but if you are going to, you better do it now." He looked at me, then at the diving board and the deep water. After much inner turmoil, he had an idea. He said, "I'll go off that diving board if you get in the water underneath it."

I was only too glad to oblige. In the time we had left, Jacob must have jumped off that board ten times. Each time I would get to him as soon as his little head bobbed to the surface and help him to the side of the pool. What made the difference for him? Having his father in the deep end with him. Now why was this so important to my six-year-old son? He believed some things about me then that, well, let's just say they are no longer a part of his teenage worldview! He believed that I was strong. (Why do they have to lose that "My daddy can do anything" mentality?) But more than that, Jacob was confident in my love for him. You'll have to take my word for this, but I have the best kids ever. I love them with all of my heart, and Jacob was confident in my love. Therefore, from his perspective, if his daddy was in the deep end, he knew he could jump off that board right into the deep water and everything would be all right.

What Jacob believed about me through the idealistic eyes of a six-year-old son are the two key characteristics that God wanted David to believe about him. In Psalm 62:11–12 David writes, "One thing God has spoken, two things have I heard: that you, O God, are strong, and that you, O LORD, are loving."

The combination of these two attributes makes this verse an essential description of our Father. If God were just strong, our feelings toward him would probably be motivated by fear. Do you remember how Dorothy and the gang felt about the Wizard of Oz at first? I'm afraid that if all I knew about God was that he was all-powerful, I would probably be cowering like the cowardly lion in his presence.

If God were just love, we might want to be with him, but we would not depend on him when a mountain needed to be moved or an enemy needed to be defeated. Remember how you felt when you first got a look at the wizard behind the voice, the lights, and the big green face? He was just a harmless old man. If God were only a kind grandfatherly being, we might want to sit on his lap, but we certainly wouldn't sleep well at night knowing that the whole universe was under his control.

But God is not either/or . . . he's both! He is strong *and* loving. Our Father spoke the word and there was light. He breathed into clay and there was man. He gave a dried-up, aged couple a good laugh and then a promised son. He plagued a pharaoh and rescued a race. He caused a fish to catch a man and a man to catch a boatload of fish. He took down a giant with a boy and a sling and fed a gigantic crowd with a boy and his lunch. He stopped the sun from setting and caused the Son to rise. Our God is absolutely strong!

God is also absolutely loving. George MacDonald describes the depth of God's love for us:

> Now what is the deepest in God? His power? No, for power could not make him what we mean when we say *God*. Evil could, of course, never create one atom; but let us understand very plainly, that a being whose essence was only power would be such a negation of the divine that no righteous worship could be offered him: his service must be fear, and fear only. Such a being, even were he righteous in judgment, yet could not be God.
>
> The God himself whom we love could not be righteous were he not something deeper and better still than we generally mean by the word—but, alas, how little can language say without seeming to say something wrong! In one word, God is love. Love is the deepest depth, the essence of his nature, at the root of all his being.[1]

God is love. Have we grown so accustomed to those words that they no longer have meaning? Have we bought into false images that are nothing more than our attempt to create God in our own image? We so often become accustomed to a picture of God that is merely a caricature of his true self. His justice is overemphasized so that he is only a stern judge eager to announce his verdict on us. He's a dutiful parole officer constantly checking to see if we have crossed the line. We assume that, like us, God has trouble forgiving. He gets to the place where he says, "I've had it up to here with you." But he's not like us. Isn't that wonderful? How have we missed that the very essence of God is love and that his steadfast love endures forever?

[He's a] . . . God who grabs scalawags and ragamuffins by the scruff of the neck and raises them up to seat them with the princes and princesses of His people.

Is this miracle enough for anybody? Or has the thunder of "God loved the world so much" been so muffled by the roar of religious rhetoric that we are deaf to the word that God could have tender feelings for us?[2]

Why did God want David to know that he was strong and loving? Why would he want you to know this? If we believe that God is strong and loving, I mean really believe it, then what is produced in us is exactly what God deeply desires from us: *Trust.* Spend some time on that word. Trust is an endangered species, quickly disappearing from our experience. Everyone knows that you can't trust anyone, right? Can't trust lawyers, can't trust government officials, can't trust the president. Can't trust salesmen or mechanics or those who handle your luggage at the airport. Can't trust your husband or your wife or the detective you hire to keep them under surveillance. Can't trust your baby-sitter, so you better hide the video camera and keep it rolling while you're gone. And above all (this one hurts), can't trust preachers!

Our family was traveling with our Coleman pop-up camper. After the second flat tire on the camper on the trip home, we were wondering about the age-old conundrum: "Why do the wicked prosper and the righteous suffer?" Since we had already used our spare, we had to leave the camper on the road and find a tire store that sells little camper tires (not as easy as you might think). We finally found one, *and* they had our size tire. But we still had a problem. (Obviously we still had some suffering, and some wicked folks still had some prospering, to do.) This was the end of our vacation, we had spent most of our cash, and it was a season in which our family had done some "plastic surgery" (we had cut up our credit cards). We had a personal check; however, unfortunately, as big as life, a sign over the register read No Checks Accepted! I was sure I could sweet-talk the guy. I explained our predicament . . . no go, he wasn't the least bit sympathetic. Finally I used the ace up my sleeve. "Sir," I said humbly, "I can certainly understand why you would have such a rule, but I want you to know that I am a pastor." He cut me off from saying anything more. Then he replied with a gleam in his eye, "You were better off before you told me that!"

Well, we left the camper on the side of the road, went home, got money, and returned the next day with a tire. The suffering was complete. You just can't trust anyone these days, not even preachers!

Trust may be endangered on earth, but it is a value in God's kingdom. God wants you to know him in face-to-face intimacy so you will see that he is essentially *strong* and *loving*. This is his essence. I minister in a town filled with academics and theologians; it can be rather intimidating. When a discussion gets too deep, I get really antsy. I have enough trouble with the easy-to-understand things about the faith. That's why I will always remember one of my seminary professors telling us about a question put to the great theologian Karl Barth. (Don't pronounce the *th;* it's just a *t* sound; if you pronounce the *th,* you'll look stupid . . . *trust* me!) He was asked, "What's the most profound theological truth?" He thought for a moment and then responded, "Jesus loves me this I know, for the Bible tells me so."

It's right in there, in the song we have known since we were very little. Jesus, God's Son, loves me. God is love. "I am weak, but he is strong." God is strong. You don't have to cower in fear; he's not just a voice, lights, and a big green face. And you can rest assured that he's in absolute control of the universe. You can do nothing

to make him love you any more. You have done nothing that has made him love you any less.

> His [God's] love is capable of transforming our cowardly,
> distrustful hearts into hearts strong in the trust that they
> are loved. We do not have to do anything, except let our
> unworthy, ungrateful selves be loved *as we are*. Trust
> *happens!* You will trust Him to the degree that you know
> you are loved by Him.[3]

Our time really is limited. This "free swim" of grace
is not going to last forever. You might as well go ahead
and jump into the deep end of trust. Two things the
Father has spoken, two things have we heard: Our God
is strong *and* loving! Come on . . . your Father is waiting, and the water is just fine!

Grace

He replied, "Whether he is a sinner or not, I don't know. One thing I do know. I was blind but now I see!"

John 9:25

"My sheep listen to my voice; I know them, and they follow me. I give them eternal life, and they shall never perish; no one can snatch them out of my hand. My Father, who has given them to me, is greater than all; no one can snatch them out of my Father's hand. I and the Father are one."

John 10:27–30

It has to be one of the best scenes in the Bible! It's all there, all the elements of a good story: heroic power and selfish power, pathos, fear, conflict, transformation, courage, and best of all, grace. The story is found in John 9:

> As he went along, he saw a man blind from birth. His disciples asked him, "Rabbi, who sinned, this man or his parents, that he was born blind?"
>
> "Neither this man nor his parents sinned," said Jesus, "but this happened so that the work of God might be displayed in his life. As long as it is day, we must do the work of him who sent me. Night is coming, when no one can work. While I am in the world, I am the light of the world."
>
> John 9:1–5

When I read this passage, I can't help but roll my eyes just a bit at the disciples. Don't you sense some awkwardness in it all? There they are with Jesus and a *man born blind.* Picture it: They are standing with Jesus, who has displayed awesome healing power again and again . . . and into the scene enters a man born blind. What do the disciples think to do? They begin a theological debate concerning the origin of his blindness. And what about their bedside manners with the sick? Can you imagine that they related his blindness to either his sin or his parents'? What a terrible burden it must have been to live in biblical times and believe that all suffering was related to personal or family sin. Certainly a case can be made even today that some sin has physical repercussions. But right there in front of the guy, a discourse of sin and suffering? What must the man born blind have felt?

If I had been writing the script, the story would have gone something like this: As soon as Peter sees this guy, his first reaction is, "Hey Jesus, we got us another one! Touch him, speak to him, show him how much you love him . . . make him see!" It is interesting how quickly Jesus moves through the theological debate to a rather pragmatic evaluation: "This happened so that the work of God might be displayed in his life." He then adds a powerful, demonstrative statement: "While I am in the world, I am the light of the world." Then things get exciting (and just a bit repulsive).

Jesus works his mouth to create a lot of saliva. He spits on the ground and makes some mud. This is where I would like just a bit more information! Did he work the ground with his fingers or did he use a stick? Did one of the disciples go, "ughhh!"? Then he puts this mud pie on the guy's face, right on his eyes. Thankfully the man born blind couldn't see it coming. After this Jesus says, "Go, wash in the Pool of Siloam" (v. 7).

The next sentence in God's Word doesn't get enough notice. It's just there. It's not red-lettered, it's not highlighted, it's not even its own verse. It's just a part of verse 7. When you think about all of the power and the emotion in this rather black-and-white verse, when you read between its lines, no, when you see it in living color . . . this partial verse deserves more credit: "So the man went and washed, and came home seeing." Isn't that awesome?! He was a man *born* blind! Go, Jesus!

Now, I've got to tell you that I don't like the way the rest of the story line goes. I would love to do a rewrite. Here's the gist of how I would direct things: The man born blind went and washed and came home seeing . . . and when he got to the gate of his hometown, the watchman couldn't believe his eyes. He was so happy! He erupted through the town with joy about his friend, his brother, who had been miraculously healed. The leaders of the church decided to have a "covered dish dinner" in his honor. Aunt Bessie made her famous fried chicken. And there was peach cobbler with Grandpa

Ned's homemade vanilla ice cream, enough for everyone to have two scoops!

It didn't happen like that though.

When the people from his hometown first get a look at him, they begin arguing among themselves about whether it is really him or someone who just looks like him. How devaluing for this guy! They ask him how this happened. He says, "This man Jesus made some mud with his spit and put it on my eyes, then told me to wash in the Pool of Siloam." It sounds even crazier coming from him, doesn't it?

The folks from his hometown decide to take the man born blind to the religious leaders. The religious leaders are not convinced that this is the same guy that was born blind. Why is it that all these folks from his hometown have such a hard time telling whether or not it's really him? I wonder if it is because this man was forced to beg to survive. I wonder if it is because everybody had stopped looking at him a long time ago. It was easier to pretend that the blind beggar just didn't exist.

It's not long before the religious leaders realize that they have some legal capital against Jesus in this man's story. The religious leaders interrogate: "You say he put mud on your eyes? Now, you're saying that this man Jesus did this today? On the Sabbath? Certainly this Jesus cannot be from God; he doesn't even keep the Sabbath!" They were referring to the asinine additions that had been made to the Sabbath laws regarding work. When they couldn't get the kind of information they wanted from the man, they decided to bring in his parents.

They continue their "bright-light-in-your-face" interrogation. "Is this your son, the one born blind? How is it that he can see?" The tension in the room was thick. The parents were very afraid. They knew that if things went badly, they could be excommunicated from the temple by these leaders. They would be ostracized in their community. They respond, "We know this is our son, but that's all. He's of age; you'll have to ask him." Dad and Mom leave their boy all on his own with these bad men.

In the man's face now, the religious leaders probe, "Give glory to God, we know this man is a sinner." Now here comes the best part of the story. The intensity has to be similar to that Tom Cruise/Jack Nicholson movie *A Few Good Men,* where Jack has this great line: "You can't handle the truth!" The man born blind, the guy who should be the center of a celebration, had been pushed and prodded by a Nazilike interrogation. Finally he's hit his limit and declares, *"Whether he is a sinner or not, I don't know. One thing I do know. I was blind but now I see!"*

Now I'm no Greek scholar. But I am just sure that we must have missed something in the original language. Certainly, immediately following this awesome line, the man born blind said under his breath: "Argue with that!" or "Interrogate that!" Now this should have shut their mouths, but it didn't. They continued in their witch hunt. The Bible says that they hurled insults at him. At one point they say, "You were steeped in sin at birth!" (v. 34). Wow! What a way to end the day after, "So the man went and washed, and came home seeing." Finally the religious leaders throw the man born blind out of the temple. How sad . . .

But here is some good news. John 10 is about Jesus being the Good Shepherd. As a foreshadowing of this grand truth, we see Jesus functioning in this role at the end of chapter 9. Jesus finds out that the man born blind has been thrown out of the temple. *And he finds him.* I love to picture Jesus looking for this man. This scene ends with Jesus making himself known to this man. (Remember, this guy had never seen Jesus!) In this wonderful encounter of grace, the man believes and worships Jesus. Now that's how this story should end!

What is the "one thing" essence of this story? This story is about the transforming power of the Lord Jesus Christ and of one who received grace. In the beginning of the story, he's a beggar, blind from birth. At the end of the story, he has encountered Jesus, been healed and transformed by grace. Every one of us should have a similar story. It doesn't have to be a rags-to-riches story, but in its essence, it should have the same dynamics. Have you had an encounter with Jesus that has transformed your life? Is "Amazing Grace" more than just a hymn to you? Is it a testimony?

> Amazing grace! how sweet the sound,
> That saved a wretch like me!
> I once was lost, but now am found,
> Was blind, but now I see.[1]

Let's take a "grace break." Go ahead and begin humming this great hymn. Get up, stretch, get another cup of coffee and maybe a cookie. Then come back to the book. I've got another story to tell you that gives a pretty good definition of grace.

Are you back? This story is one chapter earlier, John 8.

The scene begins with Jesus teaching at dawn. Stop right there. Imagine the tranquility. Jesus and some followers are up to see the sun rise and then a crowd gathers in the temple courts. Jesus begins to teach them. Talk about your "Hallmark" moment!

In the midst of wonderful tranquility comes a wicked intrusion. The religious leaders march right into the center of the moment dragging a woman caught in adultery and make her stand in front of the whole group. Now forgive me, but again I would like more information. I've led a fairly sheltered life, I know, but doesn't it usually take two to "tango"? Is this some boys' club we're dealing with here that let the man sneak out the back door? And I'm a bit repulsed that, apparently, the perpetrator must be "caught in the act." I don't like the thought of a bunch of religious leaders peering through curtains to catch this woman. Are they really concerned about justice? Or are they using this woman to get at Jesus? (I wonder if this isn't the first time that men have used her.)

This woman is dragged from the night-light to the spotlight and forced to stand in front of the group and in front of Jesus. The religious leaders reveal their evil plan: "Teacher, this woman was caught in the act of adultery. In the Law Moses commanded us to stone such women. Now what do you say?" (vv. 4–5).

Talk about a dilemma. If Jesus went along with the Law of Moses, he was breaking Roman law. If he didn't go along with the Law of Moses . . . well . . . he didn't go along with the Law of Moses! That couldn't be God! The religious leaders are licking their chops, the woman is bent over in shame, the disciples are holding their breath, and Jesus is writing in the dirt with his finger (no spit this time though).

What is he doing? Is he writing down their names, letting the religious leaders know that he knows them? Is he writing a list of their sins? Is he bent down so he can periodically look into her eyes? Is he overcome with her shame and just can't stand? We know that they continue to fire questions at him until he stands up. He's now ready to speak and you can probably hear a pin drop. "If any one of you is without sin, let him be the first to throw a stone at her" (v. 7). Then he stoops down and again writes on the ground.

Silence . . . and then the first sound—the thud of a stone hitting the ground, and then more thuds. The Bible says that one by one, from the older leaders to the younger leaders, they left the scene. Until she is standing alone with Jesus. She was taken from the night-light to the spotlight, but now she stands before the brightest light in the world. It's not over for her.

Again let me change the story line. What if it went like this . . . Jesus walked over to her and with tremendous force, threw her to the ground. Then with anger in his face, nostrils flaring, and teeth clenched, he shouted, "Harlot!" He reached for several of the dropped stones. Standing back from the trembling woman, he began to throw them at her with all of his might. Relentlessly he continued to throw each stone, each hitting the mark, causing blood to flow.

It's difficult to think of Jesus doing anything remotely like this, isn't it? I know what you are thinking: *What kind of sick mind do you have? You've watched too many of those Jack Nicholson movies, buddy!* Here's what I'm thinking. When Jesus stood up, he stated the rules: "If any one of you is without sin, let him be the first to throw a stone at her." Those were the ground rules. Now, what do we know about Jesus? He says it himself in this very chapter (John 8:46), "Can any of you prove me guilty of sin?" No one could or ever will. It's why his death was "once and for all." He was the perfect sacrifice, without a spot of sin or a blemish of iniquity. According to the rules, he could have thrown the stones. Instead he looked into the woman's eyes and said, "Woman, where are they? Has no one condemned you?"

"No one, sir," she said.

"Then neither do I condemn you" (vv. 10–11).

There it is! The definition of grace that I promised. According to the rules, he could have thrown a stone . . . but he didn't. He refused to condemn her. In fact Jesus never condemns. What about hell, you might ask? Well, it's real. But not a single person will be in hell because Jesus condemned them to be there. In fact only one sin will land you in hell. You can think of the top ten sins that anyone could ever commit. I mean the really, really bad ones. They won't condemn you to hell. The only sin that will cause anyone to spend an eternity in hell is this: to refuse the grace of Jesus Christ. Jesus doesn't condemn. His Holy Spirit convicts, but there is a huge difference between conviction and condemnation. Condemnation generates shame. It causes your spirit to be bent over. It makes you want to hide. It creates fear. The devil loves it. Conviction is so different. It enables you to see clearly. It straightens you up. It draws you in. It creates freedom. God loves it. Jesus could have condemned her, but he didn't. And he won't. That's grace!

I know what you're thinking again: *Now wait just a minute. This Jesus you have presented . . . is he soft on sin?* Let's get back to the story. Right after he says, "Then neither do I condemn you," the Bible says that he makes a declaration: "Go now and leave your life of sin" (v. 11). Let's look closely . . . he doesn't say, "I know your background, your lifestyle. When you get back to your life, try really hard not to, you know, do bad things." He doesn't say, "Wear this adultery patch and try to cut down." He says, "Leave your life of sin," period.

He calls her to holiness! This story doesn't just give us a definition of grace—he could have, but won't—it also gives us what I believe is the key to holiness. We will never be able to leave our lives of sin simply because the Bible says so, or even less, a preacher says so. The power to be holy comes from our real-life experience of receiving grace. Real holiness is our natural response to radical grace. This woman's hope for an abundant life of holiness was in her ability to live in the experience of coming from the night-light to the spotlight to the light of the world, and she was not condemned. She was offered grace.

Now that I have teenagers in my home, I look at all the angles in hope that I can provide an environment that will cause them to stay close to Jesus and not have to carry a lot of sin's baggage. I've done some inventory in my own history. Through my teenage years, I stayed pretty close to Jesus. What kept me through those turbulent years? I know that I experienced the keeping power of Christ, but there was more. I remembered specific times when faced with opportunities to sin. As a preacher's kid, I was deeply aware that my decisions could impact my father's ministry. People take great delight in telling the horror stories of past preachers' families who shipwrecked. I didn't want to hurt his ministry. But even more than that, I knew that my decision to sin would hurt his heart. I was confident of and grateful for his love. I knew that he and my mother prayed for me and cared for me. I can remember weighing the chance to sin with that reality. There was usually no contest. I didn't want to hurt his ministry or, even worse, his heart. How could I sin in the atmosphere of such love? I now see how closely this resembles my relationship with my heavenly Father and my pursuit of holiness. I don't want to hurt my heavenly Father's ministry, but even more, I know that my willful sin hurts his heart. How can I sin in an atmosphere in which my heavenly Father lavishes such love upon me?

How could this woman continue in sin in response to such "can't believe it's true" grace? Real holiness is the natural response to radical grace!

Have you come out of the night-light and stood before the light of Jesus? Have you come to terms with the fact that we all are spiritually blind from birth? If we could see what God sees, we would know that each one of us has been caught in the act of sin. Is your spirit bent over in condemnation? Please know this . . . ultimately the only power to condemn you is your refusal to receive Christ's grace! Oh, that you would encounter Jesus in such a way that you experience spiritual sight, life, healing, release, and transformation.

I love that the man born blind didn't get bogged down in the religious leaders' legal maneuvering. He didn't enter into their theological debate about Jesus' identity. In fact the man knew that he didn't know all the answers. He didn't really even know who Jesus was: "I don't know whether he is good or bad!" But there was *one thing* he knew . . . he was blind but now he could see! Have you encountered such amazing grace? Are you living in the present reality of it? Maybe you feel like you are lost. Maybe you have been the recipient of injustice at the hands of the church, tossed out and wounded. I'm not sure who actually gets credit for this statement, I think maybe Chuck Swindoll: "The church is the only institution that shoots its wounded." Sometimes those who represent Christ choose to condemn instead of trusting in the Holy Spirit's power to convict. You might have even had your parents leave you out in the cold. Please remember this good news: Jesus *is* the Good Shepherd.

There is a place of quiet rest, Near to the heart of God,
A place where sin cannot molest, Near to the heart of
God.

There is a place of comfort sweet, Near to the heart of
God,
A place where we our Savior meet, Near to the heart
of God.

There is a place of full release, Near to the heart of
God,
A place where all is joy and peace, Near to the heart of
God.

O Jesus, blest Redeemer, Sent from the heart of God,
Hold us who wait before Thee, Near to the heart of
God.[2]

Jesus is the Good Shepherd. Listen to his voice, the one that draws you in. He is saying, "I have given you eternal life, you shall never perish. My Father, who has given you to me, is greater than all; No one can snatch you out of my Father's hand. I and the Father are one."

Let this Good Shepherd find you.

Humility

Jesus looked at him and loved him. "One thing you lack," he said. "Go sell everything you have and give to the poor, and you will have treasure in heaven. Then come, follow me."

At this the man's face fell. He went away sad.

Mark 10:21

For the law of happiness in this universe seems to be: Center yourself on yourself, and you won't like yourself. Lose yourself in the needs of others, and you will find yourself—find yourself a happy person. That is the basic law of life, human and divine, in this universe. Break it and you get broken—there are no exceptions.

E. Stanley Jones

47

The voice of one crying in the wilderness: "Prepare the way of the Lord, make his paths straight. Every valley shall be filled, and every mountain and hill shall be brought low, and the crooked shall be made straight, and the rough ways shall be made smooth; and all flesh shall see the salvation of God."

Luke 3:4–6 RSV

I was raised in the church; I've graduated from a Christian college and seminary. But I missed just how radical the message of Jesus was until the last few years. You certainly get more than an inkling of the kingdom's radical nature from the above passage in the third chapter of Luke. This is how Donald B. Kraybill describes this passage in his book *The Upside-Down Kingdom:*

> John the Baptist shouted these words of Isaiah to announce the advent of Jesus. The dramatic pictures portray a revolutionary new kingdom. The Baptist describes four surprises of the coming kingdom: full valleys, flat mountains, straight curves, and level bumps. He expects radical shake-ups to accompany the kingdom. Old ways will alter beyond recognition. John warns us that the new order, the Upside-Down Kingdom, will revolutionize the prevailing social landscape.[1]

One of the recent lessons that the Holy Spirit has been teaching me is not to always trust my human instincts. In Christ's kingdom, most things are upside down. This is how Paul describes this lesson: "Do not deceive yourselves. If any one of you thinks he is wise by the standards of this age, he should become a fool so that he may become wise. For the wisdom of this world is foolishness in God's sight" (1 Cor. 3:18–19).

The next "one thing" passage is a good illustration. A part of me says, "Jesus, how in the world did you let this

48

guy get away?" The passage is found in Mark 10:17: "As Jesus started on his way, a man ran up to him and fell on his knees before him. 'Good teacher,' he asked, 'what must I do to inherit eternal life?' "

From a human perspective, this guy looks like a great catch as a disciple. Especially when you compare him with the less-than-ideal crew that Jesus picked. This man had it all! From all of the Gospel accounts, we can piece together this profile: He was a rich young ruler. He had money, manners, and morals. He had prosperity, posterity, and power. He had riches, rank, and religion. He knew how to get things done. He was a man of influence. He not only knew how to do things right, he knew how to do the right things. He was used to making an investment and getting a return. Conventional wisdom would have said, "Sign this guy up, woo this man in, make sure he's on your team. Just imagine his leadership potential . . ."

Jesus saw something in him that others couldn't see. Although with some spiritual discernment, you might be able to see a flaw from his very first question: "What must *I* do to inherit eternal life?" Certainly, this guy was used to *making* things happen. What if he's after eternal life in the same way he attained his last windfall? I believe what Jesus saw in this rich young ruler could very well be the deadliest enemy to spiritual experience—self-sufficiency.

Jesus begins his ministry to this young man. His first questions are meant to peel away the surface resistance. "Why do you call me good? . . . No one is good—except God alone. You know the commandments: 'Do not murder, do not commit adultery, do not steal, do not give false testimony, do not defraud, honor your father and mother' " (vv. 18–19).

Jesus first presents him with some of the commandments. Jesus is giving him an opportunity to become aware of his need. But true to form, the rich young ruler responds with self-deceptive pride: "No problem, I've been keeping all of these since I was a boy!" Wow! Talk about being caught red-handed. Does he know whom he is talking to? Jesus is able to look into your eyes and see your soul. This man is the child with icing on his face trying to convince his mother that it's not his fingerprint on the birthday cake. Nobody had kept the law perfectly. Paul tells us that the law was given to us so that we would know what our sins were. The young man's "no problem" answer is symptomatic of his "I've got things under control; I can handle things myself" manner.

Now here's one of the surprises of the story. Instead of Jesus snickering or using his divine leverage to humiliate this "imposter," the Bible says, "Jesus looked at him and loved him."

I don't know about you, but for all of us who have struggled with a prideful, deceptive, self-sufficient heart, that verse is wonderful! Jesus looks at him, deep within his self-sufficient soul, and loves him. Jesus, with surgical precision, continues, "One thing you lack. Go, sell everything you have and give to the poor, and you will have treasure in heaven. Then come, follow me." Okay, this is pretty radical! Granted, it must seem more radical to us than to most of the world. We have so much that we would need to liquidate. We're the culture that has to rent somebody else's garage because we no longer have enough room in our own garage, basement, and attic. But this must have been radical to the rich young ruler as well. What was Jesus thinking? This isn't a universal stipulation in Jesus' encounters with followers.

I really don't believe that the man's accumulation of money created the "one thing" that he lacked. I think Jesus' suggestion that he "sell out" and follow him was Jesus' attempt to further peel away layers of resistance and ultimately allow this man the opportunity to see his deepest need. His love of money was not the issue. It was a symptom of a greater issue: self-sufficiency. Following Jesus means giving up your ability to control, to chart your own course, to be the captain of your own soul. This guy couldn't do it. Jesus could see that and he wanted the rich young ruler to know this important truth: There is no way to save yourself! Max Lucado writes the following concerning trying to "earn" your way into heaven:

> He [Christ] doesn't say improbable. He doesn't say unlikely. He doesn't even say it will be tough. He says it is "impossible." No chance. No way. No loopholes. No hope. Impossible. It's impossible to swim the Pacific. It's impossible to go to the moon on the tail of a kite. You can't climb Mount Everest with a picnic basket and a walking stick. And unless somebody does something, you don't have a chance of going to heaven.[2]

The real answer to this guy's question, "What must I do to inherit eternal life?" is "There's nothing that you can do!" It's a matter of surrendering to what's already been done for you in Jesus Christ.

What comes next in the story is fairly unusual in the ministry of Jesus. A man has come to him, knelt before him, talked with him, and received from him. And here's what happened: "At this the man's face fell. He went away sad, because he had great wealth" (v. 22). I want to time travel back to that scene and "do something" about it. *Hey mister . . . don't go! You have no idea who you are leaving. You don't realize how empty all your "stuff" really is. Don't you realize that his love could fill the great void in your life? Jesus . . . go after him. Don't let him just walk away with his head down and his heart sad. Don't you realize how much potential he has?*

51

Again and again in parable, sermon, and act Jesus startles us. Things in the Gospels are often literally upside down. Good Guys turn out to be Bad Guys. Those we expect to receive the reward get a spanking instead. Those who think they are headed for heaven land in hell. Things are reversed. Paradox, irony, and surprise permeate the teachings of Jesus. They flip our expectations upside down. The least are the greatest. The immoral receive forgiveness and blessing. Adults become like children. The religious miss the heavenly banquet. The pious receive curses. Things aren't like we think they should be. We're baffled and perplexed. Amazed, we step back. Should we laugh or should we cry? Again and again, turning our world upside down, the kingdom surprises us.[3]

The rich young ruler doesn't see it; he just doesn't get it. He's filled with pride and can't let go. His life is centered around himself. And he's not alone in Mark's Gospel. If Hebrews 11 is a "who's who" chapter for heroes of the faith, Mark 9 and 10 read like a loser list of "kingdom wanna-bes." Let's take a brief inventory. In Mark 9:33 and the verses that follow, while Jesus and the disciples are on the way to Capernaum, Jesus asks his men what they had been arguing about. Not one of the guys speaks up, and their eyes must have darted away from Jesus in embarrassment. They had been arguing about which one of them was the greatest. Jesus had to sit them down and say, "If anyone wants to be first, he must be the very last, and servant of all" (v. 35). Then, in hopes that this would seal a truth in their minds, he brings a child to stand among them. He takes the lad in his arms and says, "Whoever welcomes one of these little children in my name welcomes me; and whoever welcomes me does not welcome me but the one who sent me" (v. 37). This would not be the last time Christ's followers would need this lesson.

Apparently, not long after this, John is in a huff! He marches right to Jesus and with disdain tells Jesus about a guy who has the audacity to be casting out demons in Christ's name. "Of course," John says, "I told him to stop because *he's not one of us.*" How Jesus maintains his composure is beyond me. After all, just a few verses ago, Jesus had to deliver a demonized boy that the disciples had worked on to no avail. Now John is telling somebody who's actually doing the stuff to stop because "he's not one of us"? Jesus looks into John's prideful eyes and says, "Whoever isn't against us is for us, John."

Then, not long after this, the disciples rebuke mothers who are bringing their children to Jesus. They believe that Jesus doesn't have time for unimportant people like these women and kids. Why won't they just leave him alone? Didn't Christ just say to them with a child in his arms, "Whoever welcomes one of these little ones, welcomes me and my Father"? Wow! What is it going to take to get them to understand?

And not long after this, James and John secretly come to Jesus and say, "Jesus, we want you to do whatever we ask."

Jesus says, "Go on."

"We want to be the ones who get to sit at your right hand and your left hand when you come into your Kingdom."

When the ten other disciples find out that James and John were vying for positions of honor, they become indignant.

All of these things happened in Mark 9 and 10! The closest people to Jesus are filled with pride and self-centeredness. It is a wonder that at this point Jesus doesn't look up to his Father and say, "Beam me up, Dad! These folks are nuts!"

Right smack dab in the center of these stories comes the rich young ruler. Doesn't *anybody* around Jesus get it? Doesn't *anybody* see? Isn't there *somebody* who understands humility? Actually, one guy in Mark 9 and 10 does. One person sees—a blind guy:

> Then they came to Jericho. As Jesus and his disciples, together with a large crowd, were leaving the city, a blind man, Bartimaeus (that is, the Son of Timaeus), was sitting by the roadside begging. When he heard that it was Jesus of Nazareth, he began to shout, "Jesus, Son of David, have mercy on me!"
>
> Many rebuked him and told him to be quiet, but he shouted all the more, "Son of David, have mercy on me!"
>
> Jesus stopped and said, "Call him." . . .
>
> "What do you want me to do for you?" Jesus asked him.
>
> The blind man said, "Rabbi, I want to see."
>
> "Go," said Jesus, "your faith has healed you." Immediately he received his sight and followed Jesus along the road.
>
> Mark 10:46–52

Finally, somebody who sees. . . . He didn't posture or primp in Christ's presence. There was no way for him to be an imposter. He had nothing to bargain with; he was a blind beggar. All he had was a sense of who Jesus was and what he could do, and he had the boldness to ask for Christ's mercy. It was enough!

At the end of what must have been a long day in the life of Jesus, he's the one guy who must have put a gleam in Jesus' eye. He knew who Jesus was, and knew how much he needed him. That's humility. The rich young ruler walked away with his head hung and his heart sad in its self-sufficiency. The blind beggar "saw" it. He cried out for mercy and walked with Jesus along the road, watching the sun set on a trying day.

Generosity

Jesus looked at him and loved him. "One thing you lack," he said. "Go sell everything you have and give to the poor, and you will have treasure in heaven. Then come, follow me."

At this the man's face fell. He went away sad.

Mark 10:21

A Christian is one who cares.

Baron Von Hugel

If you were in an ecstasy as deep as that of St. Paul and there was a sick man who needed a cup of soup, it were better for you that you returned from the ecstasy and brought the cup of soup for love's sake.

Meister Eckhart

We can dance around it, but it's still there. All through the Gospels, Jesus links eternal life with the proper handling of our wealth. Let's broaden that. Survey from Genesis to Revelation; you can't miss it. God is relentless in his intention that we understand his heart. He loves the poor, he identifies with them, he will defend them, and his ultimate desire is that his family would respond with Christlike compassion each time they see someone in need.

How did I miss such a central theme in God's Word? I grew up with a definite bent toward evangelicalism. My parents came to know Christ at a Billy Graham crusade in Philadelphia the year before I was born. I cut my teeth (literally) while my dad responded to the call to ministry by attending Asbury College and Asbury Theological Seminary, two strong evangelical schools. I watched many people get "saved" in his ministry. I wanted to follow in his footsteps. My call to ministry involved hearing the Lord say very simply but powerfully, "I want you to win as many people to Jesus as fast as you can." Now that's real ministry! I was proud to be an evangelical in what was becoming an increasingly liberal denomination. I sometimes looked down on those who were giving themselves to the "social gospel." I mean, what good is it to meet people's needs when they are on their way to hell? Andraé Crouch had it right; Michael W. Smith did too: *Jesus is the answer for the world today.* Right?

How did I become so satisfied with only a partial message? In the last decade, while experiencing the "white knuckle ride" on what John Wimber referred to as "the third wave," how did I focus on other kingdom "signs and wonders" and not include "good news for the poor"? How could so many of us wear the WWJD? bracelet and be so insensitive to what he actually did?

An old rabbi was once asked why so few people were finding God. He wisely replied that people are not willing to look that low. Jesus was born in a stable, and God is especially concerned for the poorest, the lowliest, the lost, and the neglected.[1]

Sure, the money probably wasn't the "one thing" that caused Jesus to say to the rich young ruler, "One thing you lack." But I have never preached nor heard a message on this passage that highlighted Jesus' concern for the poor. He really did say to this man, "Go, sell everything you have and give to the poor, and you will have treasure in heaven" (Mark 10:21). Certainly Jesus saw tremendous kingdom value in turning this man's wallet upside down for the benefit of those who were economically oppressed. It's one of his favorite themes.

I love the contrast in Christ's parable of the rich man and Lazarus in Luke 16:19–31:

> "There was a rich man who was dressed in purple and fine linen and lived in luxury every day. At his gate was laid a beggar named Lazarus, covered with sores and longing to eat what fell from the rich man's table. Even the dogs came and licked his sores."
>
> verses 19–21

There was a contrast in the way these two men lived and died and how they were treated in eternity.

The Rich Man	Lazarus
Rich	Poor
Purple clothes (royalty)	Beggar's rags
Owned a gated mansion	Lived at a gate
Feasted daily	Hungered daily
Family	Dogs
Lived to make a name for himself	Lived to survive
Status	Sores
Buried	Body most likely taken to the dump
Tormented in hell	Comforted at Abraham's side

What a contrast! Their lives and their deaths could not have been more different. And the contrast was eternal. You see it in Abraham's words to the rich man:

> "Son, remember that in your lifetime you received your good things, while Lazarus received bad things, but now he is comforted here and you are in agony. And besides all this, between us and you a great chasm has been fixed, so that those who want to go from here to you cannot, nor can anyone cross over from there to us."

verses 25–26

The chasm was "fixed," the die cast; no matter how strongly the rich man pleaded, their fate could not be changed. This story from Jesus not only addresses how we handle our wealth but how we treat those in need. And the eternal stakes are high! Because we live in such affluence, it is good for us to remember how Jesus wraps up his encounter with the rich young ruler: "How hard it is for the rich to enter the kingdom of God!" (Mark 10:23). Why is it so hard? Why did the rich man in this parable go to hell? William Barclay writes:

> He had not ordered Lazarus to be removed from his gate. He had made no objections to his receiving the bread that was flung from his table. He was not deliberately cruel to him. The sin of the rich man was that he never noticed Lazarus, that he accepted him as part of the landscape and simply thought it perfectly natural and inevitable that Lazarus should lie in pain and hunger while he wallowed in luxury. The sin of the rich man was that he could look on the world's suffering and need and feel no answering sword of grief and pity pierce his heart; he looked at a fellow-man, hungry and in pain and did nothing about it. His was the punishment of the man who never noticed.[2]

One lived to make a name for himself, and the other lived to survive. One more contrast stands out in this story. The beggar has the honor of being the only character in any of Jesus' parables with a name. For more than two thousand years, followers of Jesus Christ have known this man's name—Lazarus. And the rich man who lived to "make a name for himself" . . . what was his name?

Generosity. It was not only important to Jesus, but it was important in the first-century church. It may seem as if I'm going a long way to make this point, but I think it will be worth it, so stay with me. I believe a case could be made that one of the most important chapters in all of the New Testament is Acts 15. This is the chapter in which Paul and some brothers from the church in Antioch have a "showdown" with Peter, James, and the rest of the apostolic leaders in the church at Jerusalem. What was at stake was whether or not Gentiles who became Christians would have to embrace a form of Judaism as well.

The church at Antioch had experienced phenomenal growth. Through the power of the Holy Spirit and under the leadership of Paul and Barnabas, it was becoming the real headquarters of the Christian movement. The disturbance began when some "unauthorized" leaders from Jerusalem came down and began teaching that "Unless you are circumcised, according to the custom taught by Moses, you cannot be saved" (v. 1). Paul and Barnabas decided to go right to the perceived top. Along with some others, they left for Jerusalem. When they got there, they were welcomed, but immediately some of the Christians who had been Pharisees stood up and said, "The Gentiles must be circumcised and required to obey the law of Moses" (v. 5).

What would Peter and the rest of the boys do? Can you imagine how important the Law of Moses was to these early Jewish believers? Remember how repulsive the habits of the Gentiles were to obedient Jews? Could they just let Gentiles continue in a lifestyle that for generations had been an anathema to God's people? And what about the issue of control? This Antioch church was a bit of a "wild branch." Wouldn't it best serve the cause of Christ to pull in the reins just a bit? After much discussion, Peter stands. Although he is a man who loves his tradition, he reminds the leaders of how God used him to deliver the message to Gentiles and of how the Holy Spirit seemed to make no distinction between the races. Resisting his human instincts, he challenged the Jerusalem leaders not to put a yoke on the necks of Gentile believers. Peter stated with emphasis, "We believe it is through the grace of our Lord Jesus that we are saved" (v. 11).

This led to a time of testimonies from Paul and Barnabas about the saving power of Jesus among the Gentiles. When they finished, the leader of the church in Jerusalem stood. James, the blood brother of Jesus Christ, began to speak. With prophetic power he quoted from the Old Testament and then gave his verdict: "It is my judgment, therefore, that we should not make it difficult for the Gentiles who are turning to God" (Acts 15:19).

Thus the way was paved for the spontaneous expansion of Christ's kingdom. The leaders of Jerusalem refused to go with their human instincts. They willingly released the control of the church to the Holy Spirit. I believe that this decision released the church to move within a few generations from Jerusalem, to Judea, to Samaria, and to the uttermost part of the earth.

Now what does this have to do with generosity? See what Paul says about this meeting with the Jerusalem council in Galatians 2:

> For God, who was at work in the ministry of Peter as an apostle to the Jews, was also at work in my ministry as

an apostle to the Gentiles. James, Peter and John, those reputed to be pillars, gave me and Barnabas the right hand of fellowship when they recognized the grace given to me. They agreed that we should go to the Gentiles, and they to the Jews. *All they asked was that we should continue to remember the poor, the very thing I was eager to do.*

verses 8–10, emphasis added

Wow! I continue to marvel at the end of that passage. This council at Jerusalem easily rendered the most significant decision of the early church. It dealt with issues that had been important to the Jewish race since Moses. It also had the human dynamic found in any institution: the need to control. In the midst of such critical issues, at a point where the Holy Spirit seemed to be doing new things that didn't mesh with their own theology, the Christlike leaders of the early church in Jerusalem basically said to Paul, "This is not what we are called to do. The one thing that we ask of you is that you care for the poor." Do you think that ministry to the poor was of real value in the early church?

Our message and ministry in the church today is more than "getting people saved." As we pray the prayer that Jesus taught us to pray, "Thy kingdom come. Thy will be done in earth, as it is in heaven" (Matt. 6:10 KJV), and wear bracelets that ask "WWJD?", we must value what is valued in Christ's kingdom and do what Jesus actually *did!* Clearly, followers of Christ respond to those in need with generosity. Our motivation for such a lifestyle is not so that we don't wind up in hell; it's not because the poor need us; it's not because it feels so good to give. We live with this kingdom value because God identifies with the poor. His word is clear: If you want to find him, be with the poor, care for the poor. Remember the words of Jesus, "When you have done it to the least of these . . . you have done it to me."

The congregation that I pastor is filled with a generation known as "Generation X." Don't believe the press reports on these young people. They are not a listless, purposeless generation. The young men and women I am privileged to love and care for are better known as "Gen X-treme." They love Jesus with a righteous passion, worship him with reckless abandon, and are willing to give their lives for Christ's cause. I believe that they may very well be "the harvest generation," the generation that will see God's glory fill the earth and witness the blessed return of our Lord. One of the best examples of this X-treme generation is Steve and Pam English. They left our church one Sunday morning and drove their pickup truck through Mexico to Guatemala. There they founded a ministry called "The World Our Parish" and have started a home for at-risk children. As their pastor, I have been able to visit their home several times. By far the best part of the trip is to hear the stories of where these children have come from and then compare the horrors of their past with the joy of their present.

In November of 1999, the Englishes learned of a month-old baby that had been abandoned in the government hospital. Actually he had been abandoned twice. He was abandoned first by his mother, who was single and unable to provide for him. Then he was abandoned a second time by a Guatemalan couple, who when they found out that he was hydrocephalic, aborted the adoption process and left him at the hospital. A social worker brought baby Victor to the attention of Steve and Pam. The Englishes at first said no. After all, rules had been established. It was hard enough trusting the Lord to meet the needs of their other children. This baby would need so much—so much care, so many expenses. The extent of brain damage had yet to be determined.

He would certainly need neurosurgery to place a shunt to drain the building fluid on the brain down to his stomach. What would the impact be on the other children?

But the Lord kept saying to Steve and to Pam independently, "Take this child." When they visited Victor at the government hospital, they were horrified to see that those in charge refused to waste government funds on "this type" of child. The operation he needed would cost close to two hundred U.S. dollars. They were told that the funds could be better used on a child who was going to be "normal."

Steve and Pam had no idea of the battle they were facing. Agreeing to take Victor was not the end of their emotional roller coaster. They needed a doctor to release Victor from the public hospital. That was done. The next battle was not so easy. They needed a judge to give a court order to allow them to receive Victor into their home and allow him to be transferred to a private hospital to receive the "urgent" surgery. This request was given a very short answer: no! When Steve asked for a reason, he was told to come back the next day. Every minute they waited increased the chances of more severe brain damage, and eventually, the doctor had told them, Victor would die.

When Steve finally was able to see the judge, his rationale became clear. This judge was "in charge" and no "gringo" was going to tell him what to do! Steve had all of his legal papers in order; he and Pam had gathered as much prayer support as possible. If the judge would not give the order, Steve was ready to break the law and risk losing his home and being deported. He could not get away from God's word to take this child. He ached at the thought of this little boy with the oversize head and such a tiny body pushed to the back corner of the nursery, receiving no care. He looked the judge in the eye and said, "If this child dies or has any more brain damage because this surgery has been delayed, you will have to answer to God." The judge looked back at Steve and laughed. Then he called in his secretary, had her type the order, and within five minutes had signed it. Victor had his surgery, and two days later was released to the Englishes.

As the days passed, the prayers for Victor's healing increased. The other children in the home laid their hands on baby Victor and prayed. They believed for his healing with childlike faith. Eventually Victor's head stopped growing; the shunt was working. Over the next fifteen months, Victor improved, and his motor skills continued to advance. Not long ago, while the doctors were performing a procedure on Victor, they realized that his shunt was no longer necessary. Most hydrocephalic children live their whole lives with these shunts. Victor was no longer in need of it—a miracle! The doctor said to Steve, "This is very unusual. But Victor no longer needs the shunt. He's going to be a normal boy." Steve shared with the doctor and then all those who had been praying, "This isn't unusual. Our God heals."

I began writing this book while visiting Steve, Pam, and their precious children. What a joy it was to hold Victor and watch him crawl and then begin to walk. There was rejoicing as he learned to swing the plastic bat at the cloth ball that I brought for him. You should have seen how handsome he looked in the University of Kentucky Wildcat outfit my wife sent for him. What an awesome little boy!

Steve and Pam English looked low enough to see a baby twice abandoned in the corner of a public hospital in Guatemala City. They found a baby with an oversized head and an undersized future. Actually, what they found was Jesus. "When you have done it to the least of these, my children . . . you have done it to me." They responded with X-treme generosity.

Devotion

"Martha, Martha," the Lord answered, "you are worried and upset about many things, but only one thing is needed. Mary has chosen what is better, and it will not be taken away from her."

Luke 10:41–42

My greatest temptation in ministry is to attempt to do something *for* Christ before I spend time *with* Christ.

Samuel Logan Brengle

I think Martha jokingly referred to them as "Jesus and the Dirty Dozen!" The story is found in Luke 10. Jesus and his disciples visit at the home of Martha, Mary, and Lazarus in Bethany. I love to picture it in my mind, attempting to envision all of the human dynamics and emotions and add just "a little" from my own mind . . .

Martha must have seen them coming as she looked out the window by the front door—Jesus and his twelve disciples. They sure could kick up a lot of dust and who knows what else on their way to Bethany. She was thankful that they felt like her home was their home away from home. She really loved having them all there, but couldn't they wipe their feet when they came in? She quickly fluffed the pillows and arranged the magazines on the coffee table "just right," as they made their way up the pathway to the door. When the doorbell rang, she opened the door and with just a bit of a forced smile said, "Oh Jesus, and the boys . . . welcome!" She cleared her throat and with a little hesitation said these words, "Make yourselves at home."

Those were the last words she would be able to speak to them for a while. There was so much to do. As she made her way through the house, she whispered under her breath, "Why don't they ever call first!?" She was amazing; what a cleaning machine. In minutes she had all of Lazarus's dirty clothes picked up from the bathroom floor and a shine on the faucet. In record time she set the table with the special "china." Only the best for Jesus! She had already worked up a sweat when she entered the kitchen to prepare dinner. There was a roast to be cooked, potatoes to be mashed, cole to be slawed (just checking to see if you are alert!). As she walked by the archway going into the dining room, she saw her sister, Mary, out of the corner of her eye. She marched through the dining room and stood at the threshold to the living room. They were all so enthralled at what Jesus was saying that no one even noticed Martha standing there tapping her foot with her hands on her hips and beads of sweat just over her upper lip. The Bible says that she was "distracted by all the preparations that had to be made" (Luke 10:40). Finally she spoke. She spoke to Jesus because she knew that she was too angry to speak to Mary. "Lord, don't you care that my sister has left me to do the work by myself? Tell her to help me!" (Luke 10:40).

That's when it happened! Jesus said her name twice! If there's one thing for sure through the pages of Scripture, it is this: When God says your name twice, you'd better listen. Something really important always follows. "Martha, Martha," the Lord answered, "you are worried and upset about many things, but only one thing is needed. Mary has chosen what is better, and it will not be taken away from her" (Luke 10:41–42).

Jesus looked past her eyes and saw her troubled soul. His words, "you are worried and upset about many things," literally mean "you are torn in two." Jesus wanted the best for Martha.

His lesson for her was this: Don't be distracted by many good things; choose the one thing that's best!

This is a story about two women who loved Jesus and wanted to please him. One chose to do many "good" things *for* Him. The other chose what was best: being *with* him. At the beginning of this chapter is a quote from the great holiness preacher and Salvation Army officer Samuel Logan Brengle. He said, "My greatest temptation in ministry is to attempt to do something for Christ before I spend time with Christ." Sometimes I feel as though Jesus would like to stand center stage in our churches and speak with his loud voice: "Don't just do something, stand there." We live in such a busy society and have become such a busy church. It reminds me of the title of a book I read years ago, *Little House on the Freeway*. That's what we've become! We are a church torn in two. We are people distracted by so many good things, many of them good things for Jesus.

Go ahead, take a moment to do some personal inventory, take your spiritual pulse. I imagine that it is usually racing. If you have children, think about all of the good things that your kids are involved in. You know how easy it is to feel as though you are a glorified taxi driver! You are well aware of the energy it takes to make ends meet in your home. If you are married, you probably need dual incomes. And if you serve in the church, you know that most congregations have programmed the joy right out of following Jesus.

Jesus longs to look past our eyes into our troubled souls and speak our names twice. He wants to speak with authority and say, "Rich, Rich, don't just do something, stand there! Just stop. Breathe. Put that book down. Let me see your eyes. Become aware of me and my love for you." Lest you be confused, I'm not talking about whether or not you have your daily devotions. Although I treasure a daily time with the Lord, I've learned it's not so much about daily devotions as it is a heart of devotion. Jesus is looking for followers who will sit at his feet, choosing a lifestyle of devotion, time spent with him. Jesus says it's the *one thing* that is needed.

One of the most wonderful things the Holy Spirit has witnessed to my spirit is this: The Father loves me even more than all the good things I can do for him. I continually want to bring something to him so that I can prove to him that he made a good choice in choosing me. Yet the *one thing* he really wants from me is *me!* I am haunted by the passage that indicates that many will stand before his judgment throne listing all of the good and powerful things they did in his name. The Bible says that God will respond to many of them: "Depart from me . . . I never *knew* you."

I relate to the story of the father of four children who ranged in age from a teenager down to a five-year-old. One Monday work had been very stressful. His plate was full and all he wanted that evening at home was some peace and quiet. He sat in his recliner, took off his shoes, and got lost in the newspaper. The first interruption was his teenager with a math problem. He put the paper down and solved the young man's problem with him. As soon as he got positioned for peace and quiet again, the eight-year-old came in with a scraped elbow and tears. The father put down his paper, pulled the little boy up in his arms, and kissed the hurt away. When things were "all better," the child was sent on his way. It wasn't long before the eleven-year-old girl came in with an urgent request: "Daddy, the ice cream man is outside. Do you have fifty cents?" The father didn't even put the paper down; he reached into his pocket and pulled out two quarters and handed them over.

After a few more minutes, he sensed he wasn't alone in the room. He lowered the paper enough to see his five-year-old daughter standing in front of his chair looking at him. He dropped the paper with accumulated frustration and said, "What do *you* want?" The little girl replied with a great big smile, "Nutt'in Daddy, I just wanted to sit on your lap!"

That story invites the Holy Spirit to gently ask, "When was the last time you came to the heavenly Father like that?"

> Heavenly Father,
> I don't want you to solve my "problems,"
> I don't want you to heal my hurts,
> I don't want you to provide for my needs.
> I just want to "be" with you,
> to let you know that I love you.
> I just want to sit in the lap of your presence.

The one thing that is needed, the best thing of all, is to be seated with him, to be in his presence. He wants us to choose against anything that would distract us, even what many would see as "anointed service," and choose for a heart that is totally devoted to him.

That's what Martha's sister Mary did consistently. We see Mary of Bethany several times in the Gospels. And in most cases, she winds up in the same place—at Jesus' feet. That's not a bad epitaph for someone, is it? *She was the woman who spent time at Jesus' feet.* I love the scene that happens in the last week of Jesus' life. You find it in John 12:

> Six days before the Passover, Jesus arrived at Bethany, where Lazarus lived, whom Jesus had raised from the dead. Here a dinner was given in Jesus' honor. Martha served, while Lazarus was among those reclining at the table with him. Then Mary took about a pint of pure nard, an expensive perfume; she poured it on Jesus' feet and wiped his feet with her hair. And the house was filled with the fragrance of the perfume.
>
> verses 1–3

What a radical act of devotion! Several important characteristics of Mary's devotion are worth emulating. First, her gift was costly. Judas is quick to point out that what Mary was pouring onto the feet of Jesus was worth a year's wages. This was an extravagant act of love! Such an act of devotion was a testimony to Mary's faith, prompted by a revelation of spiritual understanding. Long before the disciples would "get it," Mary understood that Jesus was going to die. But she had faith to believe that his body would not need the same burial procedure given in a natural death. There was no need to save this perfume for his burial because his body would not see decay. Mary had faith to believe what had been revealed to her: Jesus would be resurrected. Mary's devotion was also clothed in humility. There were few more humble tasks than dealing with the feet of a first-century traveler. You can fill in the gaps here; we are not just talking about a little bit of dust. Mary fully identified with Jesus. As this pint of pure nard covered the feet of Jesus, Mary got herself completely involved with Jesus. She wiped his feet with her hair. This meant that they shared the same fragrance. Finally, Mary's devotion ultimately affected all those who were near her: "And the house was filled with the fragrance of the perfume."

I want to choose a lifestyle of devotion like Mary's— devotion that is costly. I want to give to Jesus the first-fruits of my love, not the leftovers. I want a life of devotion filled with faith and motivated by revelation and spiritual understanding. As Paul prayed for the church in Ephesus, I keep asking that the God of our Lord Jesus Christ, the glorious Father, will give me the Spirit of wisdom and revelation, so that I may know him better (Eph. 1:17).

I choose a devotion characterized by the humility of Christ. I want a "poorness of spirit" that continually recognizes my spiritual bankruptcy apart from the grace of Jesus. I want my lifestyle to identify me clearly as one who is with Jesus. I would like the fragrance that is on him to be the fragrance that is on me. I don't want to let anything, even good things, cause me to lose my noticeable identification with Jesus. Concerning such a loss, John Henry Jowett wrote:

> First of all, our characters will lose their spirituality. We shall lack that fine fragrance which makes people know that we dwell in "the King's gardens." There will be no "heavenly air" about our spirits. Atmosphere will not be mysteriously changed by our presence. We shall no longer bring the strength of mountain-air into close and fusty fellowships. And surely, this ought to be one of the most gracious services of a Christian minister,—by his very presence to create a climate by which the faint and overburdened are revived.[1]

I choose a lifestyle of devotion that will have a spiritual impact "on the house." I want the fragrance of Jesus on me to change the spiritual atmosphere in my home, in my church, and in my community.

While I was writing this chapter, I had the privilege of visiting the International House of Prayer (or as they refer to it, IHOP) in Kansas City. What a wonderful expression of Mary's devotion. In a very humble setting, men and women of all ages, economic positions, and races are singing and praying to Jesus twenty-four hours a day, seven days a week. They follow the pattern that is used in describing the worship that takes place in heaven around Christ's throne:

And when he had taken it, the four living creatures and the twenty-four elders fell down before the Lamb. Each one had a harp and they were holding golden bowls full of incense, which are the prayers of the saints. And they sang a new song:

"You are worthy to take the scroll
  and to open its seals,
because you were slain,
  and with your blood you purchased men for God
  from every tribe and language and people and
  nation."

Revelation 5:8–9

Heaven's worship is continual, it is musical (harps), and it is prayerful (bowls). Under the leadership of IHOP's founder, Mike Bickle, more than a hundred young men and women have left their homes, families, jobs, and even countries to come to this place. They raise their own support so that they can provide ministry as intercessory missionaries. Every day, all day, people come from the workplace, mothers come with their children, pastors come, and they sing and pray together. They pray for revival, they pray for the nations, they pray for healing, and they bask in God's love. It never stops. On the front wall of the prayer room, over whiteboards listing prayer requests, is this message: "The fire on the altar shall never go out. Lev. 6:12—Count Zinzendorf."

Like the Moravians under the leadership of Count Zinzendorf, this place has captured the atmosphere of Mary's house. There are no distractions; they pursue the presence of Jesus 24/7, and they have been doing it for almost three years now! Jesus has blessed their devotion with his fragrance. It really is true; time with Jesus is the "one thing" that is needed.

In that last week of Jesus' life, there was no way to miss it. It was in the air at the Last Supper, Gethsemane, his trial, the flogging, the way of suffering, and the crucifixion—the fragrance from Mary's extravagant act of devotion. This powerful, expensive perfume, meant to quell the stench of decaying bodies, was on him. The fragrance of Mary's faith was on him, *and* it was also on her. Anybody who had been with Jesus and then with Mary knew that they went together. They shared the same fragrance. And the fragrance of the perfume broken and poured out over Jesus became a symbol of the fragrance that lingers today—Christ's body broken and his blood poured out for the sin of the world. Both these fragrances came from a heart of devotion.

It's the one thing that is needed, and I want more of it!

Risk

I would like to learn just one thing from you: Did you receive the Spirit by observing the law, or by believing what you heard? Are you so foolish? After beginning with the Spirit, are you now trying to attain your goal by human effort?

Galatians 3:2–3

The doctrine of the Spirit is buried dynamite. Its power awaits discovery and use by the Church. The power of the Spirit will not be given to any mincing assent to pneumatological truth. The Holy Spirit cares not at all whether we write Him into our credenda in the back of our hymnals; He waits for our emphasis. When the Holy Spirit ceases to be incidental and again becomes fundamental the power of the Spirit will be asserted once more among the people called Christians.

A. W. Tozer, *The Divine Conquest*

I have always been very thankful for God the Father. What an awesome creator, sustainer, and provider. I have had a devoted love for Jesus the Son. I really believed that "while he was on the cross, I was on his mind." I have been very comfortable in the presence of the Father and Son. But the Holy Spirit . . . now he's . . . he's been more like the "weird uncle" of the Trinity. Every once in a while, like at a family reunion, you've got to deal with him and his crazy shenanigans. But I thought it best to just stay away from him.

When I left mainline denominationalism and planted an interdenominational church, I held on to a deep resistance to the things of the Spirit. I wanted to pursue more of the Holy Spirit, but I wanted it to be a controlled, comfortable release. Roland Allen, in his book *The Spontaneous Expansion of the Church*, describes where I was:

> Many of our missionaries welcome spontaneous zeal, provided there is not too much of it for their restrictions, just as an engineer laying out the course of a river is glad of some water to fill his channels, but does not want a flood which may sweep away his embankments. Such missionaries pray for the wind of the Spirit but not for a rushing mighty wind.[1]

When we started our church in Wilmore, Kentucky (the place that many in the Wesleyan/Holiness world refer to as "the Holy City"), we resisted the "charismatic" label. I can remember time and time again saying to folks when they asked for a description: "We're *open* to the Holy Spirit." When these words came out of my mouth on several occasions, I can remember holding both hands up in front of my chest. My body language spoke volumes. *He could come only so far into our fellowship.*

I loved that phrase, "We're open to the Holy Spirit." Even now as I type it, it's such a nice phrase. Unfortunately Jack Deere, in his book *Surprised by the Power of the Spirit,* ruined it for me.

> I frequently hear leaders say, "I am open to the gifts of the Spirit and to God doing healing miracles." Often people say this as though they think there is something noble about being "open." However, being open doesn't count very much with God. A person who is simply open is still a person who does not yet believe. If a non-Christian died while he was open to the possibility that Jesus may have died on the cross for his sins, that person would still go to hell. It is not being open that gets blessing from God, it is believing and pursuing what He promised. Jesus never said, "Blessed are the open." Would you give your money to a stock broker who said that he was open to making a profit with your life savings? Being open simply doesn't count for very much.[2]

Maybe the most critical spiritual experience in my life, since my conversion, was when I responded to the conviction of Jesus and repented for my sin of neglecting and resisting his Holy Spirit.

Certainly I had reasons for resisting the Spirit in my life. While growing up in my father's churches, our family had been hurt by prideful and rude charismatics. Through Asbury College and Asbury Theological Seminary's influence in my education, I became a product of the traditional Holiness doctrinal stance on issues relating to the Holy Spirit. It is my opinion that deep within the Holiness movement there is a (I know this term is strong, but I can't find a more accurate one) *prejudice* against anything that resembles Pentecostalism. In my experience, some of the smartest, most theologically grounded men I know become irrational when they speak of spiritual gifts and manifestations. I had one dialogue with a fellow evangelist at a Holiness camp meeting in the South, where with great intensity and a red face, he blasted the gift of tongues as "always from the devil." Another leader in the Holiness movement made a statement to me that I will never forget: "When a man has a charismatic experience, it severs his moral nerve." Our embrace of A. B. Simpson's much-loved mantra "Seek not, forbid not" regarding spiritual gifts helped to keep us a safe distance from the "danger" of going too far in the things of the Spirit. We certainly wouldn't want to fall into the deep end, would we? (I've since realized that it is a whole lot safer to fall into the deep end than the shallow end!)

I love my heritage and tradition. I am proud to be in the Wesleyan stream and a child of the Holiness movement. I am privileged to be able to stand on the shoulders of men and women like John and Charles Wesley, Francis Asbury, Phoebe Palmer, and Henry Clay Morrison (founder of Asbury Theological Seminary). These great heroes of the faith helped give birth and feed a lasting and world-impacting revival movement. In the summer of 2000, I was privileged to stand behind the pulpit in Wesley's Chapel in London, England. I was overwhelmed at the difference in the world through this one faithful man. I "re-upped" to be one of his preachers who were willing to "catch on fire and then watch people come to see him burn!" I am eternally grateful for the leaders within this movement who gave to me such a wonderful understanding of sanctification and modeled integrity in ministry. But it saddens me to see how our doctrine helped to create in me a resistance to the fullness of God in his precious Holy Spirit. And the more I uncover the real history of the Wesleyan revival, the more disappointed I am at how we have sterilized our beginnings, in many cases to accommodate our less-than-fiery zeal.

I was very much like the church in Galatia. They had been born again through the power of the Holy Spirit.

But now they were relying on a form of legalism. They were trusting in their own ability to be righteous. Paul reserved some of his most aggressive language for this church: "You foolish Galatians! Who has bewitched you? . . . Are you so foolish? After beginning with the Spirit, are you now trying to attain your goal by human effort?" (Gal. 3:1–3).

In my ministry, I was very glad to proclaim the Holy Spirit as an agent in our salvation. We certainly are "born of the Spirit" (see John 3). But beyond that the Holy Spirit did not play a vital role in me or my ministry. The Lord was waiting for me to give his Spirit "emphasis." This buried dynamite was awaiting my discovery.

When I repented of my inherited prejudice against the things of the Spirit, I began to see new dimensions of God's character and his power in my life and ministry. I realized how much I needed him if I was to be righteous. Just like the Galatians, I saw that my struggling in "human effort" had been foolish. I had a deep desire to be like Jesus, but I was unable to produce his character. E. Stanley Jones (one of Asbury's best!) writes:

> Then why isn't he [man] good? Because man hasn't power to put into action his innate desires for goodness. He is wicked because he is weak. His drives are too strong for him. . . . If, as Freud says, life is determined by urges in the subconscious, then nothing is more necessary than a power which can and does work redemptively in the subconscious and releases us from tensions between the conscious and the subconscious, unifying us there and making us free to develop and to be what we are made to be. This power is the Holy Spirit. . . . With our consent and cooperation the Holy Spirit works miracles where we stand helpless and baffled and beaten. We literally cannot control the subconscious by our willpower, our intellectual power, and by our emo-

tional power, all combined. That seething caldron of desires in the subconscious will only obey the Spirit who moved upon the face of chaos in the beginning and out of which came cosmos.[3]

As I grew sick and tired of what my "human effort" was producing in my life, and as I became aware of the depth of sin's darkness in the subconscious of my life, I became desperate for more than the wind of the Spirit. I knew that I needed a mighty rushing wind!

As I hungered for more of the Holy Spirit, I began to own a deeper, multidimensional understanding and experience of the Father and the Son. My love for God and devotion to Jesus were more fulfilling than ever before. I was getting to a deeper level spiritually than all of my pursuits in Bible study had ever taken me. Please don't take this as an excuse not to study the Word. The Bible is clear: "Study to show thyself approved" (2 Tim. 2:15 KJV). But the more I pursued the Holy Spirit, the more clearly I saw the limitations of my ability to rationally come to know God.

A. W. Tozer writes:

> Man's reason is a fine instrument and useful within its field. It is a gift of God and God does not hesitate to appeal to it, as when he cries to Israel, "Come now, let us reason together." The inability of human reason as an organ of divine knowledge arises not from its own weakness but from its unfittedness for the task by its own nature. It was not given as an organ by which to know God.[4]

The reason that my walk with Jesus had stayed one-dimensional was because the deepest part of our faith is what I would call "trans-rational." It is beyond our ability rationally to comprehend. Remember Paul's description of the love of Christ in Ephesians 3: It "sur-passes knowledge" (v. 19). Tozer ends his chapter by reminding us of our need for the Spirit's ability to take us deeper:

> We need to learn that truth consists not in correct doc-trine, but in correct doctrine *plus the inward enlighten-ment of the Holy Spirit.* We must declare again the mys-tery of wisdom from above. A re-preachment of this vital truth could result in a fresh breath from God upon a stale and suffocating orthodoxy (emphasis added).[5]

God was breathing new life into my spirit; it wasn't intellectual, it was illumination! And he was preparing to send more of the Holy Spirit's river into the channels we had established in our new church. The problem was, he didn't seem too concerned about ruining our defined embankments!

Over a two-Sunday period, three expressions from individuals within our body created some controversy. Needless to say, I was reluctant to go to my office that Monday morning following that second Sunday. Sure enough, several messages and appointments awaited me, focusing on these issues. Many in the church were suspicious about how far we would go with the Holy Spirit. They liked being "open" to the Holy Spirit . . . *just this far please.*

I decided to talk with each of these individuals. One young woman said, "I am finding that my love for Jesus has grown so big, I have to express it." My spirit wit-nessed with her spirit that she was right; Jesus deserved her open praise.

I talked with a young man who said to me:

> In the last week, while driving the van at work [he was a deliveryman], three times the Holy Spirit has over-

come me with an urge to pray, and each time, after I finished praying, the Lord pointed out a person on the street and said, "Go witness to them." All three times, the power of God was so strong that each of them gave their heart to Jesus!

My resistance was wearing thin!

I then talked to a young mother. I asked her, "What was happening to you?" She responded:

First, you've got to know that nothing like this has ever happened to me before! I was scared to death. But then the Lord told me that I could come out of the basement. I had felt like I was disqualified because of my past. He let me know that he loved me and wanted to use me!

The following Sunday night I confessed to the church family how uncomfortable these days had been and how "the stretch" of the Spirit was testing us. And then I shared the words of these interviews with them. The power of the Holy Spirit was in the room that night. It became a service in which many of our key leaders cried out for deeper expressions of the Holy Spirit in our body. We realized an important truth about God that night. When it comes to the Holy Spirit, our Father is not overly concerned about our comfort!

Thankfully Monday mornings are no longer dreaded in our church office. We aren't just "open" to the Holy Spirit anymore, we are pursuing the manifest presence of Jesus in worship every week. God has turned our hands so that we no longer try to keep the Spirit at a distance; we welcome him into our presence. We've decided that as a church it is foolish to rely on our human effort. We want the ever-increasing power of the Holy Spirit to flow, even beyond our embankments!

I've developed a theory about Paul's ministry in the early church about which I'm not totally convinced. I certainly wouldn't stake everything on this theory, but it has given me joy. You can keep it in the "for what it's worth" file. Here it is: *Something dramatic happened to Paul somewhere on the road between Athens and Corinth.*

We begin in Acts 17:16, where Paul is involved in head-to-head ministry with some really smart Athenians. He was deeply burdened for this city, and "he was greatly distressed to see that the city was full of idols." I've often thought how good God is that he sent Paul to Athens instead of Peter. Can you imagine? Peter would have taken a club and smashed all the idols! Paul, on the other hand, spends days reasoning with the people in the synagogue and the marketplace. He developed relationships with the Epicurean and Stoic philosophers, and they eventually invited him to speak at a special meeting place: the Areopagus (Mars Hill). The Bible says: "All the Athenians and the foreigners who lived there spent their time doing nothing but talking about and listening to the latest ideas" (v. 21).

Paul gives a masterful message. For years I highlighted Paul's procedure in Athens as *the* effective way to reach a pagan culture. He did so many commendable things—he spent time with them, he reasoned with them, and he spontaneously gave what has to be one of the most eloquent sermons in the New Testament. He starts the message with that great intro:

> "Men of Athens! I see that in every way you are very religious. For as I walked around and looked carefully at your objects of worship, I even found an altar with this inscription: TO AN UNKNOWN GOD. Now what you worship as something unknown I am going to proclaim to you."
>
> Acts 17:22–23

He continues his message, starting from creation and ending with judgment. He even is able to weave in some Athenian poetry. It is impressive! At the end of Paul's sermon, "some of them sneered, but others said, 'We want to hear you again on this subject.' At that, Paul left the Council. A few men became followers of Paul and believed" (vv. 32–34).

Now those results may not be too bad in many of our ministries. He got invited back; some folks responded. But certainly these are not results with New Testament proportions!

Paul moves directly from Athens to Corinth (Acts 18:1). In the second chapter of 1 Corinthians, Paul gives us some insight about his emotional state when he entered Corinth: "I came to you in weakness and fear, and with much trembling" (1 Cor. 2:3). Let's add to that personal description the gist of the message in his first chapter in this letter:

> For Christ did not send me to baptize, but to preach the gospel—not with words of human wisdom, lest the cross of Christ be emptied of its power.
>
> For the message of the cross is foolishness to those who are perishing, but to us who are being saved it is the power of God. For it is written:
>
> "I will destroy the wisdom of the wise;
>   the intelligence of the intelligent I will frustrate."
>
> Where is the wise man? Where is the scholar? Where is the philosopher of this age? Has not God made foolish the wisdom of the world?
>
> 1 Corinthians 1:17–20

A case certainly can be made that Paul has the people he met in Athens in mind as he writes these penetrating words. He was in contact with the greatest philosophers of his time during his stay in Athens. He stood on the hill where Socrates had stood. He had come face-to-face with the height of the world's wisdom.

In chapter 2, Paul continues:

> For I resolved to know nothing while I was with you except Jesus Christ and him crucified. I came to you in weakness and fear, and with much trembling. My message and my preaching were not with wise and persuasive words, but with a demonstration of the Spirit's power, so that your faith might not rest on men's wisdom, but on God's power.
>
> 1 Corinthians 2:2–5

I really do believe it. Something happened to Paul on the road from Athens to Corinth. I believe that in Athens he saw limited results: A few men became followers of Paul. But even more important, I believe Paul saw the danger of relying on his own gifting and eloquence. He came to Corinth with a new conviction: *to know nothing except Christ and him crucified, and to minister with a demonstration of the Spirit's power.* Somewhere on the road between Athens and Corinth, Paul left his eloquence and superior wisdom (see 1 Cor. 2:1).

Let me ask *you* just *one thing*. . . . Why are we so foolish? Why would we rather trust in our own abilities than in the resources of God's Holy Spirit? Who has bewitched us? We need the wind of the Spirit; no, we need a rushing mighty wind. We need the river of God; no, we need such a flood of his Spirit's power that our man-made embankments can't stand up against it. We need a message and ministry that *emphasizes* the Holy Spirit. He's not the weird uncle of the Trinity, and it's not enough to just be "open" to him. He can't be incidental;

he must be fundamental! He's buried dynamite! Pursuing his fullness won't be comfortable, and at times it may be "holy chaos"! But the alternative is a ministry and message limited by our gifting. I don't know about you, but I'll take the former.

Fullness

I would like to learn just one thing from you: Did you
receive the Spirit by observing the law, or by believing
what you heard? Are you so foolish? After beginning
with the Spirit, are you now trying to attain your goal
by human effort?

Galatians 3:2–3

The Holy Spirit descended upon me in a manner that
seemed to go through me, body and soul. I could feel
the impression, like a wave of electricity, going through
and through me. Indeed it seemed to come in waves and
waves of liquid love. . . . It seemed like the very breath of
God. . . . I wept aloud with joy and love; and I do not
know but I should say, I literally bellowed out the unut-
terable gushings of my heart. These waves came over
me, and over me, and over me, one after the other, until
I recollect I cried out, "I shall die if these waves continue
to pass over me." I said, "Lord, I cannot bear any more."

Charles Finney

I think Ezekiel 47 illustrates surrendering to the Holy Spirit and what it means to live in that fullness better than any other scriptural passage. In this vision given to the prophet of God is truth that brought revelation for Old Testament Israel, and also powerful revelation for the first-century church and for us today. In God's living, breathing Word, history becomes *his*tory. This passage comes directly from God's heart. It is his story for you, right now. As you read this text, ask yourself three questions about the river of God: What's the *source?* What's the *course?* And what's the *force?*

> The man brought me back to the entrance of the temple, and I saw water coming out from under the threshold of the temple toward the east (for the temple faced east). The water was coming down from under the south side of the temple, south of the altar. He then brought me out through the north gate and led me around the outside to the outer gate facing east, and the water was flowing from the south side.
>
> As the man went eastward with a measuring line in his hand, he measured off a thousand cubits [about fifteen hundred feet] and then led me through water that was ankle-deep. He measured off another thousand cubits and led me through water that was knee-deep. He measured off another thousand and led me through water that was up to the waist. He measured off another thousand, but now it was a river that I could not cross, because the water had risen and was deep enough to swim in—a river that no one could cross.
>
> verses 1–5

Please remember that last line for later: *a river that no one could cross.*

> He asked me, "Son of man, do you see this?"

Then he led me back to the bank of the river. When I arrived there, I saw a great number of trees on each side of the river. He said to me, "This water flows toward the eastern region and goes down into the Arabah, where it enters the Sea [the Dead Sea]. When it empties into the Sea, the water there becomes fresh. Swarms of living creatures will live wherever the river flows. There will be large numbers of fish, because this water flows there and makes the salt water fresh; so where the river flows everything will live. Fishermen will stand along the shore; from En Gedi to En Eglaim there will be places for spreading nets. The fish will be of many kinds—like the fish of the Great Sea [the Mediterranean Sea]. But the swamps and marshes will not become fresh; they will be left for salt. Fruit trees of all kinds will grow on both banks of the river. Their leaves will not wither, nor will their fruit fail. Every month they will bear, because the water from the sanctuary flows to them. Their fruit will serve for food and their leaves for healing."

verses 6–12

What's the Source?

As you read this prophetic vision of a heavenly river, did you notice the source? The Scripture says that the river came from under the threshold of the temple. More specifically, it was coming from under the south side of the temple, south of the altar. All through the Old Testament, the temple was the visible dwelling place of God. God's manifest presence hovered right over the ark of the covenant. The ark of the covenant was filled with powerful reminders of his provision and power—the tablets of stone on which God wrote the Ten Commandments, the jar holding heavenly manna, and the rod that blossomed. Over the ark and its golden mercy seat dwelled the "shekinah glory" of God. The water in the river came from there.

What's the Course?

Let's follow the direction of this river that came from the glory of God's presence. It starts from the south side of the temple, but it doesn't head south. The Bible says that the water turns and flows east. Later in this passage, we find not just the direction of the water but its destination. The water is headed toward the Arabah. In Deuteronomy 1:1, we see that the Arabah is a dry place or a desert. The Arabah is not the final destination of this river. Ultimately the river empties into the sea. We know from the description of this sea that it must be the Dead Sea. The course of God's river flows east into the desert and then empties into the Dead Sea.

What's the Force?

What power does this river have? The first sign of this river's power is its ability to increase in volume and velocity. It must have started as a trickle from the altar of God's presence. But as it trickled from the south side of the temple and flowed eastward, it didn't stay just a trickle. After fifteen hundred feet, the water became ankle-deep. This river of God didn't stay just a little brook; after another fifteen hundred feet, the water was knee-deep. Seeing how quickly the water was increasing, the man measured on. After another fifteen hundred feet, the water was now becoming a powerful force; it was waist-deep. But this was not the end of the increase. After another measuring of fifteen hundred feet, the water was a river of great volume and velocity, a river of tremendous force. The prophet of God said, "Now it was a river that I could not cross . . . a river that no one could cross" (Ezek. 47:5).

The force of this river is seen in another part of this passage: "So where the river flows, everything will live" (v. 9). The river transforms the Arabah, or desert place. The picture we see on the banks of this river is one teeming with life. Vegetation and trees line this river. There is much activity inside and around the water from God's dwelling place. The fish in this river now rival the fish of the Great Sea, or the Mediterranean. And where there are fish, there will be fishermen. The desert has become a resort! The force of this river is perhaps most clearly seen in its effect on the Dead Sea. It was called "dead" because the salt content was so high that nothing could live in or around it. But when the water that came from God's presence contacted the water of the Dead Sea, transformation occurred! The water became fresh!

The force of this river is also visible in the kind of life it produced. The trees along its banks were not just normal trees! The fruit of these trees never stopped producing. They were a constant source of nutrition. And the leaves from these trees were effective in bringing healing to all that came to the river. This river, directly from the manifest presence of God, increased in volume and velocity, brought transformation to the dry place and life to the dead place, and provided continual nutrition and healing. This was quite a river!

This prophetic vision from God has New Testament truth. It is a powerful picture of what would happen when God sent his Holy Spirit. As you reflect on God's promise being fulfilled on the day of Pentecost in the second chapter of Acts, ask yourself the same three questions: What's the source? course? force?

The Holy Spirit came directly from the dwelling place of God. Jesus said that after he ascended into heaven and was seated on the throne, he would send "another." Acts 2:2 says that a sound "came from heaven." The source of the Spirit was from the dwelling place of God.

What was the course of the Holy Spirit? Where did he go? Remember the words of Jesus in John 7:37? Describing the coming of the Holy Spirit, Jesus said that he would come to anyone who is thirsty. When the Spirit descended on the day of Pentecost, it was as though he came upon dead men and women. They were locked in an upstairs room for fear of their lives. Jesus was gone; they couldn't just go home. How do you start over after you've been with Jesus for three years? It seemed that life was over, until the Holy Spirit came. Then there was powerful transformation: "Where the river flows everything lives!"

And what about the force of the Holy Spirit? Jesus gave them a big clue at his ascension: "But you will receive power when the Holy Spirit comes on you" (Acts 1:8). The word for power is *dunamis* . . . that's right, "dynamite"! The Holy Spirit would come and there would be a holy explosion of life. He transforms everything he comes in contact with. He brought life, but not just life—abundant life, life teeming with more life! Dry places became bountiful; dead places came alive. The lives of those who received this power in the upper room would never be the same again. Those who had been "hiding" as dead men burst through that locked door, manifested visible signs of God's presence, and boldly spoke the truth concerning Jesus Christ. The first day, three thousand people were added to the number that followed Christ. From that point on, lame men would jump, persecutors would become proclaimers, and the good news of Jesus would spread from Jerusalem to Judea to Samaria and then to the uttermost part of the earth. This river of God's Spirit had tremendous force!

Have you come into contact with this river that comes from God? It is still flowing and it comes just as Jesus promised, directly from the heart of the Father. Jesus, in John 7, said that the prerequisite would be our thirst, no incantations, no hurdles . . . just our thirst. This easy thing has become the very thing so many of us lack. We are satisfied. We think we can get "just enough" of Jesus; enough to give us an eternal life insurance policy. We want to get into heaven, but we're okay if it is by the skin of our teeth. We appease a spiritual hunger and thirst with physical or material things that were never meant to, and never really will, satisfy us. Oh, if we would become thirsty for more of Christ's Spirit. If we would repent for living by our human effort. If we would believe this verse: "If you then, though you are evil, know how to give good gifts to your children, how much more will your Father in heaven give the Holy Spirit to those who ask him!" (Luke 11:13). The heavenly dam will break loose! He will bring life, abundant life, life that is teeming with more life! He gives spiritual food that brings strength and spiritual healing for our hurts! Everything that the river of his Spirit touches lives!

The most convicting part of this prophetic picture for the follower of Christ is that the river of God increased in volume and velocity. Our experience in the Holy Spirit is meant to do the same. Our encounter with the Spirit may start as a trickle at our salvation. We are washed, our sins are forgiven . . . Oh, the joy! But we are not meant to stay in the trickle. We are meant to move on, into the deeper things of God, deeper experiences of his love and power. We are meant to move through the ankle-deep water into the waist-deep water. Can you see how things become more risky in the Spirit? It is a pursuit of faith, and I love how the late John Wimber spelled faith: R-I-S-K!

Now here's the most important part of this divine vision. Eventually we are to get to the place in the river that "no man can cross." I believe that this is the clearest illustration of the experience of sanctification in God's Word. We get to the place in our experience with God where we can no longer control things; we know that we must move in obedience out of the waist-deep water. If we are going to continue with him, we have one choice and one choice alone: *Put our feet up and go with his flow!* This choice of surrender is risky for sure. The water at times is white, and there will certainly be some wild twists and turns. But our surrender to God's river will also take us to spiritual mountain views that can't be seen in the trickle of God's brook or even in the waist-deep water of a partial discipleship. We all must come to that place where God is a river that no man can cross. Like the man said to Ezekiel: "Son, daughter, do you see this?"

When I first developed this message years ago, I was preparing to preach at a revival meeting. I can remember sitting at my desk completing this sermon entitled "The River." I sat back and began to spiritually prepare for the congregation's response. I knew that I would call people to respond to the Holy Spirit by coming forward to the altar of the church. Because this was before the days of worship choruses, I began thinking about appropriate closing hymns of invitation. Almost immediately I thought of a hymn that I remembered from my childhood. I began humming it. *Shall we gather at the river, the beautiful, the beautiful river. . . .*

All of a sudden a righteous revolt welled up within me. I literally yelled loud enough for family members to check on me. I yelled, "No!" Immediately I was aware of one of the deepest problems in Christ's church. Many of us have become a part of the crowd who "gather at the river." We love the river of God's presence. In fact every weekend we gather up the kids, gather up the supplies, set up chairs, and bring picnic baskets along the banks of God's river. We even love to watch what happens in God's river. It's a weekly ritual to "gather at the river."

But God never intended that his river be a place where his people would *gather*. Instead it has always been his heart's desire that his children would *get in* his river. Are you there? You are meant to experience the trickle of his salvation, the washing away of your sin. But you are meant to move on! Move through the ankle-deep water of his love into the knee-deep water of spiritual disciplines. You are meant to move past the knee-deep water into the waist-deep water of spiritual service and witness. You see so much more of his beauty from there. But every one of us is meant to move past the waist-deep waters to that place in the river where "no man can cross." Have you come to an experience of God's sanctifying grace? Have you given up your ability to control? Have you put your feet up and surrendered to the flow of God? Are you at times lost in the paradox of the fear of the Lord and the wonder and beauty of his holiness?

Maybe some of you have been in the river of his Spirit but thought it was okay to swim around a bit and then get out. And now you have set up camp along its banks. You think you are just supposed to stay close to the river. Here's the problem. You won't end up where the river ends up!

Then the angel showed me the river of the water of life, as clear as crystal, flowing from the throne of God and of the Lamb down the middle of the great street of the city. On each side of the river stood the tree of life, bearing twelve crops of fruit, yielding its fruit every month. And the leaves of the tree are for the healing of the nations.

Revelation 22:1–2

95

This river that started from the dwelling place of God ends at his eternal throne. You are meant to get in and stay in so that you get where the river is going! The Bible is clear: "Without holiness no one will see the Lord" (Heb. 12:14).

Maybe you are in God's river but you have moved out of the center of his flow. In the vision in Ezekiel, there was a place in the river left for salt. It was a swamp or marsh area. The water there was somewhat stagnant. It may have moved around in circles, but it didn't move on. You may spiritually be at a place like that. Do you want to move on? Are you willing to ask Jesus for faith spelled R-I-S-K? Right now, if you are willing, you could trust Jesus to move you gently into the center of his Spirit's flow, but you will have to want to be filled with his Spirit.

> Are you sure you want to be filled with a Spirit who, though He is like Jesus in His gentleness and love, will nevertheless demand to be Lord of your life? . . . He will not tolerate in you the self-sins even though they are permitted and excused by most Christians. By the self-sins I mean self-love, self-pity, self-seeking, self-confidence, self-righteousness, self-aggrandizement, self-defense. You will find the Spirit to be in sharp opposition to the easy ways of the world and of the mixed multitude within the precincts of religion. He will be jealous over you for good. He will not allow you to boast or swagger or show off. He will take the direction of your life away from you. He will reserve the right to test you, to discipline you, to chasten you for your soul's sake. He may strip you of many of the borderline pleasures which other Christians enjoy but which are to you a source of refined evil. Through it all He will enfold you in a love so vast, so mighty, so all-embracing, so wondrous that your very losses will seem like gains and your small pains like pleasures.[1]

Here's another "one thing" essential: Let's not be foolish. Our salvation has been started by the river of the Holy Spirit, and we are meant to move on in him until we reach the river's destination. The river ends at the eternal throne of God in heaven. Shall we *not* just *gather* at the river—let's *get in* and go with his flow! It's a beautiful, a beautiful river.

Perseverance

Not that I have already obtained all this, or have already been made perfect, but I press on to take hold of that for which Christ Jesus took hold of me. Brothers, I do not consider myself yet to have taken hold of it. But one thing I do: Forgetting what is behind and straining toward what is ahead, I press on toward the goal to win the prize for which God has called me heavenward in Christ Jesus.

Philippians 3:12–14

The essential thing in heaven and earth is . . . that there should be long obedience in the same direction; there thereby results, and has always resulted in the long run, something which has made life worth living.

Friedrich Nietzsche, *Beyond Good and Evil*

You might be wondering whether or not I actually have the right to pen this chapter on perseverance. Do I have the experience? Have I really had to suffer? Let me reassure you . . . just weeks prior to writing this chapter, I drove with my wife and four children all the way across South Dakota! From Sioux Falls right through the Badlands into Rapid City. Now, unless you have driven this never-ending, wide-open, barren part of our country, you have no idea! Let me just tell you about one of the most exciting, most advertised, things on the trip. In the center of the state, there is a drugstore known for its free ice water. Sign after sign after sign beckoned us to see this *wonder!* Of course we stopped, what else are you going to do in the center of South Dakota! It *was* an awesome drugstore, and the water *was* good! And before I make some enemies from the great state of South Dakota, I must say that our family had one of our best vacations ever, camping in the Black Hills. It was absolutely breathtaking! But *getting there* was how I earned the right to write about perseverance.

It probably is a sign of midlife. I am on the verge of forty and am thinking thoughts that I have never thought before. Sometimes I forget and think I am just as "hip" as the college students I pastor. Then reality hits, like when a young married couple in our church came to me with their newborn baby and said, "Since we don't have our parents near us, would you be our baby's honorary grandfather?" Ouch! I know that I have grown up, because one of the new thoughts I keep having is how much I want to finish well. I don't want a ministry that is a flash in the pan. But even more important, I want to finish this race of being Christ's disciple with integrity, consistency, and grace. I don't want to lose ground in rebellion or selfishness. I don't even want to lose pace by being distracted. I want the prize! And I know that in order to win, I need what Nietzsche called a "long obedience in the same direction." That calls for perseverance.

Before we take a look at the apostle Paul's challenge to press on, I want to be sure that we all agree that *he* has the right to speak on this issue! Paul writes in 2 Corinthians 11:23–28:

> I have worked much harder, been in prison more frequently, been flogged more severely, and been exposed to death again and again. Five times I received from the Jews the forty lashes minus one. Three times I was beaten with rods, once I was stoned, three times I was shipwrecked, I spent a night and a day in the open sea, I have been constantly on the move. I have been in danger from rivers, in danger from bandits, in danger from my own countrymen, in danger from Gentiles; in danger in the city, in danger in the country, in danger at sea; and in danger from false brothers. I have labored and toiled and have often gone without sleep; I have known hunger and thirst and have often gone without food; I have been cold and naked. Besides everything else, I face daily the pressure of my concern for all the churches.

Okay, it's no drive through South Dakota, but it will have to do! Paul is qualified due to his own experience, not to mention the authority that comes from being appointed to write God-breathed Scripture. In the next "one thing" passage, Paul calls us to press on, to persevere, and he gives us some insight as to how to do it.

> Not that I have already obtained all this, or have already been made perfect, but I press on to take hold of that for which Christ Jesus took hold of me. Brothers, I do not consider myself yet to have taken hold of it. But one thing I do: Forgetting what is behind and straining toward what is ahead, I press on toward the goal to win

the prize for which God has called me heavenward in
Christ Jesus.

Philippians 3:12–14

The first "inspired" advice from the apostle Paul is
"forgetting what is behind." The more experience I have
in ministry, the more I am able to see the strategies of
the enemy. One of his great weapons against the children of God is guilt. Some guilt is good guilt. It makes
us conscious of our sin so that we can repent and receive
forgiveness. We really need to worry when we can sin
and not feel guilty! But many of us struggle unneces-
sarily with bad guilt or "false" guilt, burden or remorse
over sin we have already confessed and Jesus has already
forgiven. Some of us have internalized shame over sins
that have been done to us. We believe that we are dam-
aged goods; we could never win the prize.

The enemy loves to weigh us down with false guilt.
When we allow his strategy to prevail, we are paralyzed
and unable to persevere. The enemy has succeeded in
blinding our spiritual eyes to the reality of grace. "If we
confess our sins, he is faithful and just and will forgive
us our sins and purify us from all unrighteousness"
(1 John 1:9). The Bible also says that in forgiving us,
God takes our sins and throws them into the deepest
part of the ocean (Mic. 7:19). Corrie ten Boom said that
God also posts a sign that says, *No fishing allowed!*"
Paul writes that a key to pressing on is forgetting what's
behind.

Not only should we forget our past sins, but it's also
not a bad idea to forget our past successes. Now, certainly
we can learn from our former failures and victories. But
just like we can become paralyzed if we hold on to guilt
over forgiven sins, we can also become paralyzed by living in the glory of past successes. The people in the first

church I pastored lived this way. Whenever there was talk about the church, eventually someone would begin reminiscing about the glory days of the 1950s. I loved the stories at first. God moved. Many of the young people got saved. The church was renovated. Good stuff! But I grew tired of the stories and wondered if God had done anything good at all in the thirty years following that season of renewal. You and I can do the same thing. Our walk with Jesus can become a yellow-paged memory book of past glory instead of a present-tense experience of Christ's presence and power.

The enemy also loves to keep us from persevering by paralyzing us with defeat caused by suffering. In fact as I scan the history of Christianity, it seems that *the* key to being able to press on is a right perspective in the midst of suffering. Charles Spurgeon writes:

> Any fool can sing in the day. When the cup is full, man draws inspiration from it; when wealth rolls in abundance around him, any man can sing to the praise of a God who gives a plenteous harvest. . . .
>
> It is easy to sing when we can read the notes by daylight; but the skillful singer is he who can sing when there is not a ray of light to read by . . . who sings from his heart, and not from a book that he can see, because he has no means of reading, save from that inward book of his own living spirit, whence notes of gratitude pour out in songs of praise. . . . It is not natural to sing in trouble. . . . Songs in the night come only from God; they are not in the power of man.[1]

The Bible is clear: Suffering will come to those who follow Christ. Jesus told us to be ready. Paul wrote in Philippians 3:10–11, "I want to know Christ and the power of his resurrection and the fellowship of sharing in his sufferings, becoming like him in his death, and so, somehow, to attain to the resurrection from the dead."

The enemy would like us to see suffering as a road-block to pressing on; Jesus would like suffering to become a catalyst for greater Christlikeness!

I am undone by what I see in Acts 12. It begins with a glorious story of Peter's miraculous escape from prison. Peter was asleep in a cell between two soldiers. He was bound with two chains and sentries stood guard at the entrance. Suddenly an angel appeared; there was a great light shining in the cell, but ol' Peter was a heavy sleeper. The angel had to kick Peter in the side to wake him up! (I'm not making this up. Look for yourself.)

The angel said, "Get up," and the chains immediately fell off Peter. Peter was still a bit groggy. The angel had to tell him to put on his clothes and sandals. Then the angel had to tell him to wrap his cloak around himself and follow him. I'm getting the idea that the angel had the same experience with Peter as my wife has when she tries to get our six-year-old to dress herself! *"Peter . . . problem solved . . . get your head in this! This is a jail break!"* The angel and Peter walked right past the prison guards. When they reached the iron gate leading to the city, it just opened up! When they had walked the length of one street, the angel left Peter and suddenly Peter was "in the game." The Bible says that he came to himself. Good!

While all this was happening, in a house not too far from the jail, the church was praying. All night they had been praying for Peter's release. Peter went to the house and knocked at the outer entrance. Now this has to be one of the great scenes in all of the Scriptures. The ser-vant girl, Rhoda, came to answer the door. When she realized it was Peter, she ran right back into the house to tell all those who were praying. But she left Peter standing at the gate!

When she announced to the praying group that Peter was at the door, they replied, "You're out of your mind!" (v. 15). Isn't that wild? They had been specifically praying for Peter's release. When they were told that God had answered their prayers, they thought the bearer of the news was out of her mind. Thank goodness the Bible says that Peter kept knocking. Finally someone must have let the poor guy in. Can you imagine the celebration?

One day while I was reading this story, the Lord said, Find John. So in my mind's eye, I looked for him in this scene. Here's what I saw: John was one of the first to see Peter. His first reaction was jubilation! But then for just a moment, there was a piercing in his heart. There was deep sadness and the pain of lament. You see, in the beginning of this chapter, there is some terrible news.

> It was about this time that King Herod arrested some who belonged to the church, intending to persecute them. He had James, the brother of John, put to death with the sword. When he saw that this pleased the Jews, he proceeded to seize Peter also.
>
> Acts 12:1–3

Certainly, even if it was just for a fleeting moment, John felt what any of us would feel. *Why? Why, Jesus? Why was Peter miraculously released and my brother killed by the sword?* John must have missed his brother dearly. These two boys grew up fishing with their father, Zebedee. They left the family and the family business together to follow Jesus. Together they were known as "the Sons of Thunder." And now James was gone, brutally martyred for his faith.

This suffering could have become a roadblock for John. His "why?" could have paralyzed him from moving on. We know otherwise. John would persevere longer than any other disciple. All of the original twelve disciples except John experienced a martyr's death. John, on the other hand, persevered right through old age and exile on an island called Patmos. This "lover" of Christ's church was such a threat that the enemies of Christianity thought they would give John a punishment worse than death by exiling him. This elderly apostle pressed on so faithfully that ultimately his friend Jesus "showed up" and gave him the final revelation in God's Word! His suffering became a catalyst for greater Christlikeness.

Listen to his words in the first chapter of the Revelation: "I, John, your brother and companion in the suffering and kingdom and patient endurance that are ours in Jesus, was on the island of Patmos because of the word of God and the testimony of Jesus" (v. 9).

Recently I had the privilege of being reunited with one of our students who left Wilmore to minister in another place. While she had been a student at Asbury and a part of our church family, she honored me by letting me walk with her through some of her initial healing from years of physical abuse from her father. The stories were horrifying, but God's grace was even more beautiful in her. I was heartsick when I heard that she had been diagnosed with Crohn's disease. Apparently this disease causes your immune system to think that your digestive system is the enemy and seek to destroy it. Doctors have no real cure. This disease causes her to go through much pain; it disrupts every aspect of her life. And about every six months, it lands her in the hospital for a ten-day stay.

I was able to visit with her in her new ministry location. After we caught up, I asked her to tell me how she was doing so that I could pray for her more effectively. She said the Lord had taken her through a lot of emotions. At one time in the hospital, she realized how similar the feelings of this disease were to the feelings she had as a child being abused. After an attack, she would survey the damage and see the bruises. She would never know when the attack was coming or when the next one would follow. She was dealing again with the why questions and all of the feelings associated with being a victim.

She also told me of the struggle of faith she had been through. Was there just not enough faith for her to be healed? Was God not really who he says he is? Then she began sharing what God had given her. She said:

> I choose to believe that God is who he says he is. I believe that he is head over heels in love with me. And I also believe that it is his nature to heal. The fact that I have not been healed even though it is his nature to heal has triggered a kind of romantic mystery in me. If he loves me and his nature is to heal, and he hasn't healed me . . . then it is costing him something for me to suffer. Why would he do this? There must be some part of me that he wants and doesn't have yet, or there must be some part of him that I am not aware of yet. There's got to be something I need, because it costs him for me to suffer.

I was undone by the depth of this young woman's relationship with Jesus and her perspective in suffering. I think that she has already received a portion of the prize Paul was after! She is forgetting what's behind *and* straining toward what is ahead. She is a living illustration of Paul's word in Romans 8:18: "I consider that our present sufferings are not worth comparing with the glory that will be revealed in us."

Another key in persevering is to "strain toward what is ahead." What is ahead for you? I'm not really prophetic, but let me give it a shot. I believe that each one of you will face pain or pleasure, hurt or healing, worry or wonder, the mundane or the miraculous, defeat or deliverance, tragedy or triumph. Some of you might spend more time on the pleasure side; others may live on the pain side. Some of you will seem to skip from one miraculous mountaintop to the next. Others of you will seem to march on and on and on, right through the valley of the mundane. Like Peter, some of you may see doors swing wide open. Like James, others of you may see the swing of the sword. What's the deal?

Here's what I've concluded: When we get the pleasure, healing, wonder, miraculous, deliverance, or triumph, we should *rejoice in praise.* And when we get the pain, hurt, worry, mundane, defeat, or tragedy, we should *rest in promise.* His promises are what we strain toward; they *are* what is ahead! He won't ever leave us; nothing can separate us from his love; we can cast our cares upon him because he cares for us. He really is head over heels in love with us; he lavishes his love on us. It costs him when we suffer. He's preparing a place for us where there will be no more sin and suffering; there will be no more cancer, divorce, abuse, poverty, church splits; there will be no more tears and no more death.

Therefore, brothers and sisters, press on. Seize the day. Win the prize . . . it's your heavenward calling. But don't do it in your own human effort. Even perseverance is a gift of grace. Let him help you.

I will never forget Cora.[2] During the season in my life when I traveled as a United Methodist evangelist, I had the privilege of developing a relationship with several small churches on the East Coast. Each year for about five years, I led in a week of ministry. I would preach in the evenings and lead a community Bible study in the mornings. One year, in the morning Bible study, I taught on the Beatitudes from Matthew 5. Cora was faithful to attend each day. The final morning of our study, I finished the teaching on "Blessed are those who are persecuted" with a story about Corrie ten Boom. As I told this story, Cora began to cry. When I closed with prayer, the presence of the Lord remained heavy in that place. You could hear a pin drop. While basking in the glory of his presence, I kept my eyes shut. When I opened them, I realized I was alone in the room now with Cora.

What followed is beyond any earthly treasure. With tears still in her eyes, Cora said, "I'm going to tell you some things that I have never told anyone else."

I moved over three chairs to be next to her. She continued:

> Although my family was not Jewish, because we were from Poland and were Christian, we were taken to a Nazi concentration camp. I spent from the time I was twelve to the time I was seventeen in that horrible place. You can imagine what happened to young girls there. . . .

Cora then recounted some stories that were extremely painful for her to remember. She kept her head down as she described the horror, except for when she removed her glasses to wipe the tears from her eyes.

> Toward the end of the war, four other teenage girls and I decided to escape. In the night, we broke free of the camp and ran through the woods. Ultimately the guards caught up to us and took us back. For our punishment, they broke both our legs. We spent the remaining months of the war in our bunks until the American servicemen carried us out.

I lost all ability to provide any "professional" counsel. I sat there weeping and angry. Finally I looked at Cora and asked, "How did you do it? How did you survive?" I will never forget the strength and conviction in her response. With her head up and her eyes clear, she said, "It was the *felt* presence of God." And she stressed the word *felt*.

That's really the key, isn't it? It's how we press on in a world that is sometimes wracked with pain, persecution, and paradox. Our only hope in persevering is that he will be with us.

> But now, this is what the LORD says—
>   he who created you, O Jacob,
>   he who formed you, O Israel:
> "Fear not, for I have redeemed you;
>   I have summoned you by name; you are mine.
> When you pass through the waters,
>   I will be with you;
> and when you pass through the rivers,
>   they will not sweep over you.
> When you walk through the fire,
>   you will not be burned;
>   the flames will not set you ablaze.
> For I am the LORD, your God,
>   the Holy One of Israel, your Savior."
>
>   Isaiah 43:1–3

So, brothers and sisters, do this one thing . . . press on! Forget what's behind and strain toward what's ahead. Don't be paralyzed by sin or slowed down by distraction. When you get to sing in the daylight, rejoice in praise! When you willingly sing in the night, rest in promise. Run to win your heavenly prize. But don't run alone. He will be with you.

Readiness

But do not forget this one thing, dear friends: With the Lord a day is like a thousand years, and a thousand years are like a day. The Lord is not slow in keeping his promise, as some understand slowness. He is patient with you, not wanting anyone to perish, but everyone to come to repentance.

But the day of the Lord will come like a thief. The heavens will disappear with a roar; the elements will be destroyed by fire, and the earth and everything in it will be laid bare.

Since everything will be destroyed in this way, what kind of people ought you to be? You ought to live holy and godly lives as you look forward to the day of God and speed its coming.

2 Peter 3:8–12

Finish, then, Thy new creation;
Pure and spotless let us be:
Let us see Thy great salvation
Perfectly restored in thee:
Changed from glory into glory,
Till in heav'n we take our place,
Till we cast our crowns before Thee,
Lost in wonder, love, and praise.

Charles Wesley

It happened one afternoon while I was in the sixth grade. Several nights before, I went with the church youth group to see a movie titled *A Thief in the Night*. It was an "in your face" movie about the second coming of Jesus Christ and it shook me! When I got home from school that afternoon, I thought it was, literally, the end of the world.

The parsonage we lived in was just across the street from my elementary school. Every afternoon I would come home to find my mother waiting for me. One afternoon a few days after viewing the film, I entered the back door and went into the kitchen. My mother wasn't there, but signs of her presence were all over. The radio was on, a cookbook lay open on the kitchen table, the mixer was out on the counter, and there was dough piled on wax paper. I searched through the rest of the house, but she was nowhere to be found. When I was sure that the house was empty, I looked in the yard. It was as vacant as the house. I crossed over to the church where my father pastored. He was almost always in his office in the afternoon. I looked through the window of his office. His desk light was on, and a book was opened at his desk. I went to the front door of the church, and it was locked.

By this time my pulse was racing. I was putting two and two together. This could be it—the rapture! I beat my fist against the front door of the church and, although I didn't mean to, I broke the window on the door.

I sat on the back steps of our house crying. I really thought that I had blown it—Jesus had returned and my family was gone. It turned out that a dear family in our church had an accident and both my parents rushed to be with them. They hadn't been raptured after all; it was just much later in the day than they realized. All was well!

One day, however, it *will* be like that! Peter begins this passage about "the day of the Lord," or the second coming of Jesus Christ, with these urgent words: "Don't forget this one thing . . ." He has ministered a vast amount of truth into the church throughout his apostolic career. In this letter written toward the end of his life, he says emphatically, "There's one thing that you *must* remember . . . Jesus *is* coming back!"

How was Peter so sure? The simplest answer is that he saw Jesus go up! In Acts 1, Peter saw Jesus ascend into heaven. Can you just imagine? Jesus is right there promising dynamite power when the Holy Spirit comes, and then, like a hot-air balloon when the ropes are cut— "up, up and away!" There he goes! I wonder if anyone tried to grab on to his feet. Peter was a part of the crowd that had their mouths open so wide their chins hit their shoes. The angels who appeared probably had to clear their throats a couple of times to get everyone's head out of the clouds: "[Ah . . . excuse me . . .] Men of Galilee . . . why do you stand here looking into the sky? This same Jesus, who has been taken from you into heaven, *will come back* in the same way you have seen him go into heaven" (Acts 1:11, emphasis added).

This truth became the heartbeat of the early church. It is one of the most often repeated themes in the New Testament. The leaders of the New Testament church and the early believers were certain that Jesus was coming back. I doubt that they had the same confusion many of us have. I grew up "pre-trib" (pre-tribulation), although I never knew that I was pre-trib. I didn't know there was a label like that for what I had learned to believe, and I didn't know that there were so many alternative beliefs about the second coming. Then I got royally messed up in a college eschatology class. It seemed I changed my mind with each newly presented line of thinking. Now when I start to think about all of the charts and references to Daniel, I realize I'm not sure whether or not I'm pre-trib anymore. Instead I just get "per-turbed"! I really don't know what to think!

My guess is that the early believers didn't spend a whole lot of time trying to figure it all out. They saw him go up, and the angels started singing that old '70s song *"What goes up, must come down."* And that was it. He's coming back! My hat goes off to those who spend a lot of time in the intricacies of eschatology. Yet for me, three simple truths are found in this "one thing" passage in 2 Peter 3 that are the most important: (1) our time is short, (2) our Father loves us, and (3) we ought to be holy.

> But do not forget this one thing, dear friends: With the Lord a day is like a thousand years, and a thousand years are like a day. The Lord is not slow in keeping his promise, as some understand slowness. He is patient with you, not wanting anyone to perish, but everyone to come to repentance.
>
> But the day of the Lord will come like a thief. The heavens will disappear with a roar; the elements will be destroyed by fire, and the earth and everything in it will be laid bare.
>
> Since everything will be destroyed in this way, what kind of people ought you to be? You ought to live holy and godly lives as you look forward to the day of God and speed its coming.
>
> 2 Peter 3:8–12

Our Time Is Short

The first simple truth is this. No matter how you look at it, we just don't have a lot of time. When I felt called to full-time ministry as a college sophomore, I heard the inward, audible voice of the Lord. I had been struggling with God about my future. I wanted to be a lawyer and had refused to consider ministry. I was at a new place where I wanted Jesus more than anything else. As I prayed concerning my future, I heard the Lord say, *"I want you to win as many people to Jesus as fast as you can."* That was real! Two shifts took place in my life. First, I became burdened for those without Christ. I think the Lord gave to me just a portion of what he feels concerning the lost. I began to see people as eternal beings, and according to the Bible, most of them were on a broad road that leads to hell. I also felt a deep sense of urgency. Jesus was coming back, and I believed that it would be in my lifetime. There was no time to play games.

I've since grown up a bit. I'm not as sure that his return will be in my lifetime, but I've concluded that there is no harm in living as though it will. It's a win/win. If he does return while I'm alive, I will not have wasted any time. And if he doesn't return in my lifetime, well, I will not have wasted any time! In 2 Peter it's clear. If we could pull ourselves out of earth time and live according to heaven's clock (if it had one!), we would know that from God's perspective, a thousand years are like one day! We just don't have a lot of time.

Our Father Loves Us

Second, God loves us so much that he doesn't want to lose even one of us. Peter wants to be sure that we won't misinterpret God's patience with indifference. Just because he hasn't come yet, don't get lulled into a false sense of security. Just because so many seem to be getting away with evil, or getting away with living life as the captains of their own souls, don't let that cause you to neglect Jesus as your Lord. Earlier in chapter 3, Peter reminds us that there will be many scoffers in the last days reminding us that the promise hasn't come, that everything remains the same, nothing will ever change. Peter says, "Don't buy it! Don't let his patience be a stumbling block. He is not wanting anyone to perish; he wants everyone to come to repentance."

C. S. Lewis helps us understand the mind of God:

> Why is God landing in the enemy-occupied world in disguise and starting a sort of secret society to undermine the devil? Why is He not landing in force, invading it? Is it that He is not strong enough? Well, Christians think He is going to land in force; we do not know when. But we can guess why He is delaying: He wants to give us the chance of joining His side freely. . . . God will invade. But I wonder whether people who ask God to interfere openly and directly in our world quite realize what it will be like when He does. When that happens, it is the end of the world. When the author walks on to the stage the play is over.[1]

Christ will invade this earth. Like a thief, he will come unexpectedly. As you read this passage in Peter, certainly you get a sense of earth's finality: "The heavens will disappear with a roar . . . the earth and everything in it will be laid bare." Our Father's deep desire is that not one of us perish in the midst of his judgments and the earth's destruction. He longs to be our rescuer, our Savior.

We Ought to Be Holy

The third simple truth is that in the face of the coming end, we ought to be holy. "Since everything will be destroyed in this way, what kind of people ought you to be?" There's no doubt about it! This passage triggers some fear. I believe that it is a "holy fear." Peter is so convinced of Christ's return, the urgency of the time, the Father's heart, and the earth's coming destruction, he basically says, "People, don't mess around. Don't be caught with your spiritual pants down! It's all true. He's coming back! We gotta be ready!"

Although "holy fear" is pretty compelling, we can find an even stronger spiritual pull toward holiness and godliness as we wait for Christ's return. In 1 John, just a breath or two before we are told, "How great is the love the Father has lavished on us" (3:1) we find this verse: "And now, dear children, continue in him, so that when he appears we may be confident and unashamed before him at his coming" (1 John 2:28).

The compelling thrust of this verse and many others pulls us toward holiness from another angle. In order to get the best perspective on this truth, we have to remember that one of God's favorite images regarding how we relate to Christ is that of a bride and groom:

> As a man rejoices over his new wife, so your God will rejoice over you.
>
> Isaiah 62:5 NCV

> He has covered me with clothes of salvation and wrapped me with a coat of goodness, like a bridegroom dressed for his wedding, like a bride dressed in jewels.
>
> Isaiah 61:10 NCV

"Let us rejoice and be glad
and give him glory!
For the wedding of the Lamb has come,
and his bride has made herself ready."

Revelation 19:7

I don't think that I would ever actually do this; it would be a nasty prank. Here's the scene. One of the things I like to do before I officiate at a wedding service is to pray with the groom and his best man, and then just prior to the ceremony, I go to the bride and pray with her and the other women in the party. What if, after looking at the bride just moments before the ceremony was about to begin, I got a strange look on my face and said to her, "You're not going out there like that, are you?"

That would be terrible, wouldn't it?

I would never really do that, really! Hours have been spent preparing. Truckloads of supplies have usually been brought into the church as the women in the bridal party primped, pulled, posed, preened, and pampered. Usually three or four people are there just for the bride. And by the time the organ is ready to hit that first chord of the processional, she is ready! Only one thing is more enjoyable than watching that bride come down the aisle, and that's watching the groom watch the bride come down the aisle!

Not long after I married Tania, I wrote these words as a part of a song for her:

The day we got married, all my dreams came true.
I was standing at the altar, just waiting for you.
I saw you all in white, with your veil and bouquet.
With a tear in my eye, I just wanted to say:
 I do, I do, take you as my wife;
 To love, provide, protect, confide

'Til death leads into life.
From this day forward I'll love you more,
Sick or healthy, rich or poor.
We're bound together, so much in store!
I do take you as my wife.

When she walked down that aisle . . . well, words just aren't sufficient. I'll rest in the hope that if you are married you know what I'm talking about!

Peter writes, "Do not forget this one thing. . . . The day of the Lord will come. . . . Therefore we ought to live holy and godly lives." John writes, "Dear children, continue in him, so that when he appears we may be confident and unashamed before him at his coming."

A day is coming when we will take our place as Christ's bride. He will give the nod for the processional to begin, and the trumpet will sound. When he returns for his bride, the consummation will begin and *we will know him fully and be fully known by him*. Then, the eternal wedding party will begin!

Our task is to be ready. You might be thinking, *I don't have anything to wear. I can't go down that heavenly aisle in these rags!* Remember, he wants to cover you in clothes of salvation and wrap you with a coat of goodness . . . like a bride dressed in jewels (Isa. 61:10). It's not about you fretting and worrying about being ready. It's about you resting in what he has done and will do in you. Let him dress you in these essentials: eternity, trust, grace, humility, generosity, devotion, risk, fullness, perseverance, and readiness.

My . . . don't they make us beautiful! Words just aren't sufficient . . .

"A Benediction"

In the process of writing this book, I came across a wonderful prayer by Søren Kierkegaard. It may take a while to dig past the thees and thous, but you will find some spiritual gold! Before you turn the last page of this book, let this relevant prayer serve as your benediction.

Father in Heaven!
  What is a human being without thee! What is all that one knows, vast accumulation though it be, but a chipped fragment if one does not know thee! What is all striving, could it ever encompass a world, but a half-finished work if one does not know thee: thee the One, who art one thing and who art all! So may thou give to the intellect, wisdom to comprehend that one thing; to the heart, sin-

cerity to receive this understanding; to the will, purity that wills only one thing. In prosperity may thou grant perseverance to will one thing; amid distractions, collectedness to will one thing; in suffering, patience to will one thing. Oh, thou that givest both the beginning and the completion, may thou early, at the dawn of day, give to the young person the resolution to will one thing. As the day wanes, may thou give the older person a renewed remembrance of the first resolution, that the first may be like the last, the last like the first, in possession of a life that has willed only one thing. Alas, but this has indeed not come to pass. Something has come in between. The separation of sin lies in between. Each day, and day after day something is being placed in between: delay, blockage, interruption, delusion, corruption. So in this time of repentance may thou give the courage once again to will one thing. True, it is an interruption of our ordinary tasks; we do lay down our work as though it were a day of rest, when the penitent (and it is only in a time of repentance that the heavy-laden worker may be quiet in the confession of sin) is alone before thee in self-accusation. This is indeed an interruption. But it is an interruption that searches back into its very beginnings that it might bind up anew that which sin has separated, that in its grief it may atone for lost time, that in its anxiety it might bring to completion that which lies before it. Oh, thou that givest both the beginning and the completion, give thou victory in the day of need so that what neither a burning wish nor determined resolution may attain to, may be granted in the sorrowing of repentance: to will only one thing.[1]

A Time for Reflection

Lesson 1: Eternity

1. Think about a time early in your life when the idea of eternity became a reality for you.
2. Is God your "home," or just a "Sunday bungalow"?
3. Is this true for you: "The closer I get to God, the more intense my longing for him becomes"?
4. What phrase from Psalm 91 speaks most powerfully to you?
5. Have you ever had an experience where earthly time seemed to not exist and you "stepped into eternity"?

Lesson 2: Trust

1. Think of an experience you have had in which you had to completely trust another person.
2. Has your experience in your family, this culture, or the church made it easier or more difficult to trust?
3. What areas in your life today need to be released into the hands of our loving and powerful Father in heaven?
4. How do you feel about this quote: "You will trust him to the degree that you know you are loved by him"?
5. What is keeping you on the diving board and out of the deep end of trust?

Lesson 3: Grace

1. Can you think of other biblical characters who experienced personal suffering that led to shame? Are there any people like that in your life experience?
2. Describe the difference between conviction and condemnation.

3. What are some of the ways that Jesus Christ has made a difference in your life?
4. When you hear the word *holiness,* what do you think of?
5. Take a moment to reflect on this phrase: "Real holiness is the natural response to radical grace!"

Lesson 4: Humility

1. Think of a person in our culture or your life who reminds you of the rich young ruler.
2. What are some ways people try to inherit eternal life on their own?
3. What are the self-sufficient areas of your life?
4. Think of the very best things that you bring to Christ's table. Does he need them?
5. Try building on this quote: "Humility is knowing who Jesus is, what he can do, and how much you need him."

Lesson 5: Generosity

1. What do you think about the quote from Meister Eckhart at the beginning of this chapter?
2. Do your life circumstances or choices cause the poor to be only a part of the landscape of your life?
3. What life experiences have you had in which you encountered the poor?
4. Can you find things in your life that indicate your desire to make a name for yourself?
5. What does it mean to say, "God identifies with the poor"?

Lesson 6: Devotion

1. With whom do you have more of a natural affinity, Mary or Martha? Why?
2. List the many good things you have done in the last week for your spouse, your kids, your friends, or yourself.
3. How much time have you spent with Jesus in the last week?
4. Can you remember the last time you came to Jesus without any problems, hurts, or needs . . . you just wanted to be with him?
5. Would you like to be the kind of person in which the faint and overburdened are revived by your presence? Would you pray for the fragrance of Jesus to come on you in such a profound way that the spiritual atmosphere is changed in your home, church, and community?

Lesson 7: Risk

1. Draw a timeline for your life experience with the Holy Spirit.
2. Has the Holy Spirit been given emphasis in your life? Why or why not?
3. Do you at times feel like your spiritual life is driven by human effort?

4. Have you had experiences with the Holy Spirit in which it seemed that God was not overly concerned with your level of comfort?
5. What might be keeping you from asking God for a mighty rushing wind?

Lesson 8: Fullness

1. What do you think about when you read Charles Finney's account of being filled with the Holy Spirit?
2. Would you say that you are thirsty for more of the Holy Spirit?
3. Where are you in the river—bank? trickle? ankle? knee? waist? the river no one can cross?
4. What are the hindrances in your life that would keep you from getting to the place where you could put your feet up and go with his flow?
5. Are there any "self-sins" you need to confess? Go ahead and dive in to the deep end of trust again. . . . He is still loving and powerful. . . . He is still right there.

Lesson 9: Perseverance

1. What are some things you have had to endure that may have given you authority to speak on perseverance?
2. Have you or do you ever struggle with false guilt?
3. Have you ever spent too much time camping out in past successes?
4. What is the biggest "why?" in your life? Has it been a roadblock?
5. Why is this statement so critical: "It costs Jesus for me to suffer"?

Lesson 10: Readiness

1. Do you have any false-alarm rapture stories?
2. How has a sense of urgency regarding Christ's return affected your life?
3. Why might it be important to God that we join his side freely?
4. Make a list of all the wonderful things that must be true if Jesus is our groom.
5. Knowing that the heavenly wedding processional could begin at any moment signaling Christ's return, what things in your life would you like to let go of? What things would you like to acquire?

Notes

Lesson 1
1. Max Lucado, *The Great House of God* (Dallas: Word, 1997), 4.

Lesson 2
1. George MacDonald, *Creation in Christ*, quoted in Reuben P. Job and Norman Shawchuck, *A Guide to Prayer for Ministers and Other Servants* (Nashville: Upper Room, 1983), 168.
2. Brennan Manning, *Abba's Child: The Cry of the Heart for Intimate Belonging* (Colorado Springs: NavPress, 1994), 53–54.
3. Brennan Manning, *Ruthless Trust* (San Francisco: HarperSanFrancisco, 2000), 178.

Lesson 3
1. Hymn, John Newton, "Amazing Grace." This beloved hymn was written by Newton, a former slave trader who was transformed by the power of Christ.
2. Hymn, Cleland B. McAfee, "Near to the Heart of God."

Lesson 4
1. Donald B. Kraybill, *The Upside-Down Kingdom* (Scottdale, Pa.: Herald Press, 1990), 17.
2. Max Lucado, *The Applause of Heaven* (Dallas: Word, 1990), 30.
3. Kraybill, *The Upside-Down Kingdom*, 24.

Lesson 5
1. Harvey and Lois Seifert, *Liberation of Life*, quoted in Reuben P. Job and Norman Shawchuck, *A Guide to Prayer for Ministers and Other Servants*, 181.

2. William Barclay, *The Gospel of Luke* (Philadelphia: Westminster Press, 1975), 214.

Lesson 6

1. John Henry Jowett, *The Preacher: His Life and Work* (New York: Harper & Brothers Publishers, 1912), 58.

Lesson 7

1. Roland Allen, *The Spontaneous Expansion of the Church* (Grand Rapids: Wm. B. Eerdmans, 1962), 12.

2. Jack Deere, *Surprised by the Power of the Spirit* (Grand Rapids: Zondervan, 1993), 154.

3. E. Stanley Jones, *The Reconstruction of the Church—On What Pattern?* (Nashville: Abingdon Press, 1970), 23.

4. A. W. Tozer, *The Divine Conquest* (Harrisburg, Pa.: Christian Publications, Inc., 1950), 78.

5. Ibid., 84.

Lesson 8

1. A. W. Tozer, *The Divine Conquest,* 123.

Lesson 9

1. Charles Spurgeon, *Sermons*, vol. 2, 169–70, quoted in Elizabeth Ruth Skoglund, *Bright Days, Dark Nights* (Grand Rapids: Baker Books, 2000), 154.

2. I have changed her name for privacy.

Lesson 10

1. C. S. Lewis, quoted in Philip Yancey, *The Jesus I Never Knew* (Grand Rapids: Zondervan, 1995), 251.

Postscript

1. Søren Kierkegaard, *The Prayers of Kierkegaard,* quoted in Reuben P. Job and Norman Shawchuck, *A Guide to Prayer for Ministers and Other Servants*, 211–12.

Rich Stevenson is the founding pastor of Great Commission Fellowship in Wilmore, Kentucky. This church is committed to "fulfilling the Great Commission through a new generation." God is using this church to equip radical followers of Jesus Christ to go into all the world with a heart for the lost and a passion for God. Rich is also the leader of Great Commission Churches, International. This is a "network for the spontaneous expansion of the church." God has used this network in planting numerous new churches around the world.

Rich is a graduate of Asbury College and Asbury Theological Seminary. He served as a United Methodist pastor in the Southern New Jersey Conference for five years, and for three years as a general evangelist in the United Methodist Church through the Francis Asbury Society in Wilmore, Kentucky.

Rich has been married to Tania (Moore) since 1982, and they have four great children: Zachary, Jacob, Jessica, and Corrie.